Yoshoku
Contemporary
Japanese

A cookbook is the result of an amalgamation of talent, skill and passion.

First of all, I would like to thank Kay Scarlett and Juliet Rogers for believing in the project; Zoë Harpham, Kim Rowney and Marylouise Brammer for their editorial and design expertise; and all the behind-the-scenes stars at Murdoch Books who make it all happen.

Thanks also to Mikkel Vang and Christine Rudolph for doing an amazing job with the photography, and a huge hug to Ross Dobson for making the food look so beautiful. To Vicky Harris and Lee Husband, thank you for all your help and discriminating palates. Thank you also to Hannah Yiu and Cindy Buitenhuis from Oriental Merchant for supplying such wonderful Japanese food products.

And, finally, a very big thank you to my Japanophile mum (who still allows me to take over her fantastic kitchen from time to time), Adam, Ness, Andrew and all the rest of my wonderful family and friends for your love, support, encouragement and willing taste buds.

My dad loved his food, as I do—this is for you

First published in 2005 by Murdoch Books Pty Limited.
This edition published in 2011.

Murdoch Books Australia
Pier 8/9, 23 Hickson Road, Millers Point NSW 2000
Phone: +61 (0)2 8220 2000 Fax: +61 (0)2 8220 2558

Murdoch Books UK Limited
Erico House, 6th Floor North, 93–99 Upper Richmond Road
Putney, London SW15 2TG
Phone: +44 (0)20 8785 5995 Fax: +44 (0)20 8785 5985

Photographer: Mikkel Vang
Stylist: Christine Rudolph
Art direction and internal design: Marylouise Brammer
Cover design: Tania Gomes
Project manager: Zoë Harpham
Editor: Kim Rowney

Text copyright © Jane Lawson.
Design and photography copyright © Murdoch Books Pty Limited 2005

National Library of Australia Cataloguing-in-Publication entry
Author: Lawson, Jane, 1968-
Title: Yoshoku / Jane Lawson.
Edition: 2nd ed.
ISBN: 978-1-74266-137-7 (hbk.)
Notes: Includes index.
Subjects: Cooking, Japanese.
Dewey Number: 641.5952

IMPORTANT: Those who might be at risk from the effects of salmonella poisoning (the elderly, pregnant women, young children and those suffering from immune deficiency diseases) should consult their doctor with any concerns about eating raw eggs.

CONVERSION GUIDE: You may find cooking times vary depending on the oven you are using. For fan-forced ovens, as a general rule, set the oven temperature to 20ºC (70ºF) lower than indicated in the recipe. We have used 20 ml (4 teaspoon) tablespoon measures. If you are using a 15 ml (3 teaspoon) tablespoon, for most recipes the difference will not be noticeable. However, for recipes using baking powder, gelatine, bicarbonate of soda (baking soda) or small amounts of cornflour (cornstarch), add an extra teaspoon for each tablespoon specified.

The Publisher thanks Archaeos, Bison Homewares, Kris Coad, Moss Melbourne, Mud Australia, Simon Johnson and The Essential Ingredient for their assistance with the photography for this book.

Printed by 1010 Printing International Limited, China

Yoshoku
Contemporary Japanese

Jane Lawson

photography by Mikkel Vang
styling by Christine Rudolph

MURDOCH BOOKS

contents

japanese food western style

Writing this book has enabled me to combine two of my greatest passions—food and Japan. I've been travelling to Japan for over 20 years and it never ceases to amaze me how dramatically and quickly things there can change—yet, at the same time, there is such awe-inspiring and humbling respect for tradition. Old and new stand side by side in all facets of life. Although this could suggest confusion and contradiction, the Japanese have successfully mastered the skill of unifying the old world with the new.

Japanese cuisine is no exception: at one end of the scale is the very formal and exquisite *kaiseki* cuisine in which food is painstakingly prepared for special occasions; and at the opposite end of the spectrum lie the fast-food joints. In between these two extremes resides an eclectic mix of Buddhist vegetarian specialities; street food; *izakaya*, the Japanese version of the tapas bar; super-fresh sushi and sashimi turned out by hole-in-the-wall vendors; simple, rustic homestyle fare; and the most fantastic array of foreign food restaurants I have ever seen. Incredibly, no matter where you dine you can be assured that, in every instance, flavour, appearance, freshness and texture are of utmost importance.

Although I love the dining diversity of Japan, I am most intrigued by *yoshoku* —a magical blend of Japanese and Western ingredients and cookery methods, resulting in an array of exciting and delicious new dishes.

My aim in this book is to show just how comfortably Japanese and Western flavours can be blended. Traditional Japanese cuisine can be a little intimidating for some; however, this gentle introduction to Japanese foods will allow you to explore some less familiar ingredients with a buffer of better known flavours and cookery methods. To help familiarize you with these ingredients I have included a comprehensive glossary, which lists both the English and Japanese names, as well as suggestions for substitutes, where applicable.

Another of the really lovely aspects of Japanese cuisine is that as well as being delicious it is often very good for you. Soy and seaweed products are already highly regarded in health arenas but within these pages you will find some wonderful new ingredients, many of which are loaded with antioxidants, vitamins and minerals.

The recipes in *yoshoku* range from homey comfort food to fabulous party fare. Start in the *small plates* chapter for a range of dishes for sharing, either as a snack or en masse at a cocktail party; or select just a few for an interesting, casual dinner. Each chapter moves from lighter foods through to more substantial fare, so you can choose dishes to suit your mood. If you make a hearty selection from the *main plates* or *bowl food* chapters, perhaps start with something from the lighter end of *small plates*. *Side plates* will provide you with a little something extra to go with your mains. And finally, *sweet plates*, dedicated to a group of Japanese co-workers who once tried to convince me that we all have a second stomach reserved exclusively for dessert.

I hope you enjoy discovering *yoshoku*, and that my recipes inspire you to experiment and develop your own.

Jane Lawson

small plates

Green soya beans in the pod, known as *edamame* in Japanese, are available fresh when in season, and frozen when not. I always keep a packet in the freezer as they are so quick to prepare when unexpected friends drop in. Here, the *edamame* are served while still warm; in summer, try them chilled and serve with an ice-cold Japanese beer.

edamame

1 teaspoon dashi granules

3 teaspoons Japanese soy sauce

2 teaspoons mirin

1 teaspoon sesame oil

3 small red chillies, cut in half lengthways

4 garlic cloves, bruised

2 star anise

500 g (1 lb 2 oz) frozen soya beans in the pod

sea salt flakes

serves 4–6 as a snack

Put the dashi granules, soy sauce, mirin, sesame oil, chilli, garlic, star anise and 1 litre (35 fl oz/4 cups) water in a large saucepan and bring to the boil over high heat. Cook for 5 minutes to infuse the flavours.

Add the soya beans and cook for 2–3 minutes, or until tender. Drain well, remove the chilli, garlic and star anise, reserving some chilli and star anise for garnish, if desired. Sprinkle with sea salt and toss to combine. Serve warm in a bowl, topped with the garnishes, if using. To eat, simply squeeze the beans straight from the pod into your mouth. Supply an extra bowl for the empty pods.

hint: If using fresh soya bean pods, prepare them by rubbing the pods with salt between your hands to remove the fine hairy fibres. You will need to increase the cooking time to 6–8 minutes.

Forget the potato chips—hand around a bowl of these crunchy, nutty snacks. Lotus root is thought to increase stamina and make your skin glow—the perfect party food.

zen party mix

vegetable oil, for deep-frying
125 ml (4 fl oz/½ cup) sesame oil
200 g (7 oz) fresh lotus root
2 x 85 g (3 oz) tins ginkgo nuts, drained well and
    patted dry
300 g (10½ oz) tin cooked soya beans, drained well
    and patted dry
2 tablespoons dried wakame pieces
2 sheets of kombu, each 5 x 18 cm (2 x 7 in),
    wiped with a damp cloth, cut widthways into
    1 cm (½ in) strips
caster (superfine) sugar, to sprinkle

serves 4 as a snack

Fill a deep-fat fryer or large saucepan one-third full with vegetable oil and add the sesame oil. Heat to 180°C (350°F), or until a cube of bread dropped into the oil browns in 15 seconds.

Peel the lotus, then slice it very thinly using a Japanese mandolin or a sharp knife and steady hand. Deep-fry the lotus in three batches until golden, stirring occasionally—this will take about 2 minutes per batch. Drain well on paper towels, sprinkle with salt and set aside.

Prick the ginkgo nuts with a skewer or halve them, as they have a tendency to 'explode' when fried, then deep-fry all at once for 3–4 minutes, or until golden. Remove from the oil, drain well, and set aside in a bowl. Add the soya beans to the oil and cook in three batches for 5 minutes, or until crisp and golden. Remove, drain well, sprinkle with salt and add to the ginkgo.

Add the wakame and kombu and cook for about 30 seconds, or until the oil stops bubbling, then remove, drain well and sprinkle with a little salt and caster sugar. Allow to cool slightly, then add to the ginkgo and soya beans. Add the lotus and toss gently to combine. Taste for seasoning and add a little more salt, if needed. Serve immediately.

If making ahead of time, allow to cool completely, then store in an airtight container. If they lose their crispness, spread out on a baking tray and heat for 10 minutes in a 180°C (350°F/Gas 4) oven until crisp again.

hint: If fresh lotus root is unavailable, it is also sold thickly sliced and frozen, and in vacuum packs. Cut into 5 mm (¼ in) thick slices and increase the cooking time to 8 minutes.

The following three dressings each make enough for 24 oysters, so if you choose to serve two or three dressings at once you'll need to decrease the quantity of each.

oysters with japanese flavours

24 freshly shucked oysters, chilled

ponzu dressing
2 teaspoons lemon juice

2 teaspoons lime juice

2 teaspoons Japanese rice vinegar

1½ tablespoons Japanese soy sauce

2 teaspoons mirin

1½ tablespoons drinking sake

½ teaspoon caster (superfine) sugar

5 x 2 cm (2 x ¾ in) piece of kombu, wiped with
    a damp cloth, cut into strips

2 teaspoons bonito flakes

tiny slivers of lemon or lime zest, to garnish

wasabi dressing
2 teaspoons wasabi paste

60 ml (2 fl oz/¼ cup) Japanese rice vinegar

½ teaspoon caster (superfine) sugar

2 teaspoons mirin

1 tablespoon cream

flying fish roe, to garnish

ginger and sesame dressing
1½ teaspoons finely grated ginger

1 teaspoon caster (superfine) sugar

1 tablespoon Japanese soy sauce

1½ tablespoons Japanese rice vinegar

1½ tablespoons drinking sake

½ teaspoon sesame oil

toasted sesame seeds, to garnish

makes 24

To make the ponzu dressing, put all the ingredients, except the zest, in a non-metallic bowl and stir until the sugar has dissolved. Cover with plastic wrap and refrigerate for 24 hours. Strain through muslin (cheesecloth) or a fine sieve before using.

To make the wasabi dressing, combine all the ingredients, except the fish roe, in a bowl, whisk until smooth, then chill.

To make the ginger and sesame dressing, combine all the ingredients, except the sesame seeds, in a bowl, whisk until smooth, then chill.

Serve the oysters chilled, drizzle with one of the dressings and top with the appropriate garnish. Alternatively, serve all three dressings in separate bowls and with little spoons so guests can then select their preferred dressing.

hint: If flying fish roe, *tobiko*, is unavailable, use the larger salmon roe.

If you like nori-wrapped rice crackers, you'll absolutely love these. They are so easy to make and deliciously crisp and savoury.

nori, sesame and parmesan pastries

2 sheets frozen butter puff pastry

2 tablespoons nori flakes

2 tablespoons toasted sesame seeds

100 g (3½ oz/1 cup) finely grated
   Parmesan cheese

½ teaspoon caster (superfine) sugar

½ teaspoon sea salt flakes

50 g (1¾ oz) butter, melted

makes about 32

Lay the pastry sheets out on a bench and allow them to thaw. Combine the nori flakes, sesame seeds, Parmesan, sugar, sea salt and a little freshly ground black pepper, then divide the mixture between two small bowls.

Put one sheet of pastry on a piece of baking paper and brush the pastry with melted butter, then sprinkle with two-thirds of the mixture from one of the bowls. Press down to adhere then, using the baking paper, fold the pastry in half, from left to right, and press down again. Brush the top of this with a little more butter and sprinkle with the remaining third of the topping mixture so it covers the pastry evenly. Fold in half again lengthways so that you have a long rectangular log, and press down to adhere.

Repeat with the remaining pastry sheet and the remaining mixture. Lay the two pastry logs on a tray and refrigerate for 30 minutes. Meanwhile, preheat the oven to 200°C (400°F/Gas 6).

Remove the pastry logs from the refrigerator and, using a sharp knife, trim the ends, then cut across into 1 cm (½ in) slices. Place the slices, cut-side up, on three baking trays lined with baking paper, spacing them a little apart to allow for expansion.

Cook for 15 minutes, or until puffed and golden. Serve warm with drinks such as the Dirty ninja saketini (page 47), or as an accompaniment to Corn potage (page 69).

This dressing is quite piquant but still allows the lovely fresh flavour of the fish to shine through.

salmon sashimi with caper dressing

500 g (1 lb 2 oz) sashimi-grade salmon (in one piece)
1½ tablespoons salted capers, rinsed well and drained
2 small handfuls mitsuba or flat-leaf (Italian) parsley
½ teaspoon wasabi paste
1 teaspoon caster (superfine) sugar
1½ tablespoons drinking sake
1½ tablespoons mirin
1½ tablespoons lemon juice
mustard cress, to garnish (optional)
salmon roe, to garnish (optional)

serves 4–6 as a starter

Using a sharp knife, and carefully wiping the blade with a damp cloth between each slice, cut the fish along its length into two even rectangular blocks, then cut into 5 mm (¼ in) slices across the width. The rectangles should be about 6 x 2–3 cm (2½ x ¾–1 ¼ in).

Arrange the sashimi in a single line on a platter, with the pieces overlapping slightly or, alternatively, divide the sashimi between individual bowls. Cover and refrigerate while you make the dressing.

To make the dressing, finely chop the capers and mitsuba, then add the wasabi, sugar, sake, mirin, lemon juice and a pinch of salt and mix to combine well. Pour the dressing over the salmon and top with a few sprigs of mustard cress and little clumps of roe, if using. Serve immediately.

Wonderfully garlicky and rich with salty miso, this dip is perfectly complemented by crisp, cooling cucumber.

miso garlic dip with cucumber

1 tablespoon red miso

1½ tablespoons white miso

2 garlic cloves, crushed

2 teaspoons caster (superfine) sugar

½ teaspoon sesame oil

1 tablespoon sake

2 teaspoons mirin

large pinch of dashi granules, dissolved in
    60 ml (2 fl oz/¼ cup) hot water

4 small, chilled Lebanese (short) cucumbers, cut
    lengthways into eighths, seeds removed

serves 4–6 as a snack

Combine the red and white miso, garlic, sugar, sesame oil, sake, mirin and dashi and whisk until smooth. Refrigerate for 1 hour to thicken slightly and to allow the flavours to develop.

Serve in a small bowl with the cucumbers for dipping. (You can use other vegetables such as blanched baby carrots, asparagus spears, snow peas (mangetout) and sticks of daikon, but cucumbers are the most refreshing.)

hint: Add 40 g (1½ oz/¼ cup) finely chopped toasted almonds or peanuts to the dip for extra crunch.

Simply cooked in the shell with butter and soy sauce, the delicate flavour of these scallops is enhanced by a fresh herb and lemon dressing.

scallops with herb dressing

40 g (1½ oz) butter, melted

3 teaspoons Japanese soy sauce

¼ teaspoon sesame oil

24 large white scallops without roe, on the shell, beards removed

herb dressing

3 handfuls mitsuba or flat-leaf (Italian) parsley, finely chopped

4 shiso leaves, finely shredded

2 teaspoons finely grated lemon zest

2 garlic cloves, finely chopped

1 tablespoon toasted sesame seeds

1 tablespoon Japanese soy sauce

1 tablespoon mirin

2 tablespoons lemon juice

2 tablespoons Japanese rice vinegar

makes 24

are just cooked and the butter is a little browned—the scallops should still yield slightly to the touch. Remove from the griller and top each scallop with the herb dressing. Serve immediately.

hint: The herb dressing can also be served over grilled chicken or steak, or over other seafood.

To make the herb dressing, use a *suribachi* (ribbed mortar) or a mortar and pestle to grind the mitsuba, shiso, lemon zest, garlic and sesame seeds to a rough paste, then stir in the soy sauce, mirin, lemon juice and vinegar. Preheat the griller (broiler) to high.

Combine the melted butter, soy sauce and sesame oil and brush it liberally over the scallops, being careful not to get any on the shell. Put the scallops under the hot griller for 1½–2 minutes, or until they

Although they look similar to frittata, these are based on the traditional Japanese recipe, *chawan mushi*, steamed savoury custard cups. The steaming promotes a silken texture and is normally done in bamboo steamer baskets, but the method used here is also effective.

steamed mushroom custards

20 g (¾ oz) butter

1 teaspoon sesame oil

1 leek, thinly sliced

150 g (5½ oz/3 cups) shiitake mushrooms, stems discarded, caps thinly sliced

100 g (3½ oz/1⅓ cups) enoki mushrooms, ends trimmed, then lengths halved

½ teaspoon dashi granules

4 eggs

3 egg yolks

185 ml (6 fl oz/¾ cup) cream

1½ tablespoons mirin

2 teaspoons Japanese soy sauce

ground white pepper

Japanese mayonnaise, to garnish

snipped chives, nori flakes or bonito flakes, to garnish

soy caramel (optional)

1 tablespoon mirin

1½ tablespoons caster (superfine) sugar

1½ tablespoons Japanese soy sauce

makes 24

Put the butter and sesame oil in a small frying pan over medium heat. Add the leek and cook for 3 minutes, or until the leek has softened. Add the shiitake and a pinch of salt and cook for 8 minutes,

or until softened. Add the enoki and cook for a further 1 minute to wilt. Sprinkle the dashi into the pan and mix until dissolved. Allow to cool.

Put the eggs, egg yolks, cream, mirin and soy sauce in a bowl and beat until combined. Season with a little salt and white pepper, then strain into a bowl with a pouring lip. Place a roasting tin half-filled with water on the bottom shelf of the oven and preheat to 140°C (275°F/Gas 1).

Divide the mushrooms between 24 non-stick mini muffin holes, then carefully pour over the egg mixture. Lightly tap the tray on the bench to bring any air bubbles to the surface. Leave the custards to sit for 10 minutes then, using a fine skewer, pop any obvious bubbles.

To make the soy caramel, if using, combine the mirin, sugar and 1 tablespoon water in a small saucepan over medium–high heat. Stir until the sugar has dissolved, then bring to the boil. Cook for 2–3 minutes, or until slightly syrupy, then add the soy sauce and cook for a further 3–4 minutes until syrupy again. Cool to room temperature.

Place the custards on the middle shelf of the oven and cook for 13–15 minutes, or until just set. They should still be slightly wobbly to the touch but there should not be wet patches on top. Remove from the oven and allow to cool slightly in the tin before carefully removing.

Allow the custards to cool to room temperature, then top with a small dollop of the mayonnaise, drizzle with the soy caramel and sprinkle with chives, nori flakes or bonito flakes, or alternate with two or more toppings.

melon frost

½ honeydew melon
125 ml (4 fl oz/½ cup) Midori melon liqueur
125 ml (4 fl oz/½ cup) drinking sake
4 long strips of lemon zest, tied into knots

serves 4

Peel the melon and cut the flesh into small cubes. Put the melon in the freezer for 20 minutes, or until frozen, then put the frozen melon in a blender, along with the Midori and sake and blend until smooth. Divide between four cocktail glasses and serve with a little knot of lemon zest.

cherry blossom

185 ml (6 fl oz/¾ cup) chilled plum wine
125 ml (4 fl oz/½ cup) chilled drinking sake
250 ml (9 fl oz/1 cup) peach juice
250 ml (9 fl oz/1 cup) sour cherry juice

serves 4

Combine all the ingredients, then divide between four tall glasses filled with some ice cubes.

hint: If you can't find sour cherry juice, double the amount of peach juice.

citrus sawaah

1 pink grapefruit
1 lime
1 orange or blood orange
125 ml (4 fl oz/½ cup) shochu or drinking sake
chilled soda

serves 4

Juice the grapefruit, lime and orange, then divide between four tall glasses filled with some ice cubes. Add the shochu to each glass, then top up with chilled soda and stir gently.

hint: A popular way of serving this refreshing drink is to give guests a selection of halved citrus fruits and a hand juicer, and they simply add as much of the juice of their choice as they like. Lemons are also a popular ingredient.

lychee muddle

40 fresh lychees
125 ml (4 fl oz/½ cup) shochu or drinking sake
½ vanilla bean, split in half lengthways and
    finely chopped, or a few drops of pure
    vanilla extract
1 small handful mint leaves, torn if large
chilled soda (optional)

serves 4

Peel the lychees and remove the seeds over a bowl to catch any juices. Divide the lychees between four sturdy tumblers. Divide the shochu, vanilla and mint leaves between the glasses, then crush the lychees with a wooden spoon or muddler until the lychees are pulpy and the juice has released. Add a little crushed ice to each and serve as is or top up with soda. This is also great with a dash of pure ginger cordial.

From left: Lychee muddle, Cherry blossom.

This recipe is loosely based on two recipes: Italy's *insalata caprese*—a mozzarella, tomato and basil salad; and Japan's *hiyayakko tofu*—a chilled tofu dish. The flavour of the rich, sweet tomatoes teams beautifully with the creamy, cold tofu.

chilled tofu with roasted tomatoes

350 g (12 oz) cherry tomatoes on the vine

6 garlic cloves, unpeeled

60 ml (2 fl oz/¼ cup) olive oil

sea salt flakes

½ teaspoon caster (superfine) sugar

600 g (1 lb 5 oz) silken firm tofu

good-quality balsamic vinegar, to drizzle

sesame oil, to drizzle

3 shiso leaves, finely shredded

serves 4–6 as a starter

Preheat the oven to 160°C (315°F/Gas 2–3). Leaving the tomatoes on the vine, put them, along with the garlic cloves, in a small baking dish. Pour over the oil and sprinkle with sea salt and sugar. Put in the oven and cook for 30–35 minutes, or until the tomatoes start to shrivel slightly. Remove from the oven and cool to room temperature.

Cut the tofu into eight even slices and arrange the slices on a serving platter. Top with the roasted tomatoes and garlic and spoon over any olive oil left in the baking dish. Drizzle with a little balsamic vinegar and sesame oil and scatter the shiso over the top. Serve immediately and ask your guests to squeeze over a little of the roasted garlic, straight from its skin, if they desire.

This tempura strays a little from conventional style in that it uses a combination of two ingredients: prawns and mushrooms. Lightly cloaked in a delicately crisp tempura batter they are very hard to resist.

shiitake and prawn tempura

400 g (14 oz) raw prawns (shrimp), peeled and deveined

1 egg white

¼ teaspoon finely grated ginger

1 teaspoon Japanese soy sauce

1 teaspoon mirin

1 spring onion (scallion), finely chopped

pinch of ground white pepper

20 g (¾ oz/⅓ cup) Japanese breadcrumbs

24 medium shiitake mushrooms

vegetable oil, for deep-frying

125 ml (4 fl oz/½ cup) sesame oil

tempura batter

325 ml (11 fl oz) iced water

50 g (1¾ oz/¼ cup) potato starch, sifted

90 g (3¼ oz/¾ cup) plain (all-purpose) flour, sifted

¼ teaspoon baking powder

¼ teaspoon salt

dipping sauce

⅛ teaspoon dashi granules, dissolved in 2 tablespoons boiling water

2 teaspoons mirin

3 teaspoons Japanese soy sauce

makes 24

Roughly chop the prawns and place in a food processor, along with the egg white, ginger, soy sauce, mirin, spring onion and white pepper and process until minced. Stir in the breadcrumbs, then cover and chill for 1 hour to allow the flavours to develop and the mixture to firm up.

Discard the stems from the shiitake and fill the caps with the prawn mixture, smoothing over the top with the side of a butter knife. Place in a single layer on a tray lined with paper towels, cover with plastic wrap and refrigerate until ready to use.

To make the dipping sauce, combine all the ingredients and leave to cool to room temperature.

Fill a deep-fat fryer or large saucepan one-third full with vegetable oil and add the sesame oil. Heat to 180°C (350°F), or until a cube of bread dropped into the oil browns in 15 seconds.

The delicate tempura batter must be made quickly just before cooking. Put the iced water in a chilled bowl, add the sifted flours, baking powder and salt, all at once, and give just a few light strokes with a pair of chopsticks to loosely combine. There should be flour all around the edges of the bowl and the batter should be lumpy but not thick.

Sprinkle the prawn side of the mushrooms with a little flour and dip each mushroom into the batter to coat, then lower into the oil. Cook in batches—you'll need to do it in about six batches—so you don't crowd the pan. Cook for 2–3 minutes, or until lightly golden and cooked through. Thin the batter with a little more iced water if necessary—you should have a crisp, lacy, almost see-through batter. Serve immediately with the dipping sauce.

hint: Instead of serving the tempura with dipping sauce, serve with small lemon wedges and sprinkle with green tea salt made from ½ teaspoon green tea powder mixed with 2 teaspoons table salt.

This refreshing Japanese vinegared crab salad is a wonderful filling for these Vietnamese-style rice paper rolls. If crabs are not available, prawns are just as delicious.

rice paper rolls filled with crab salad

1 kg (2 lb 4 oz) cooked blue swimmer crab
   or other small, sweet crab—you'll need about
   400 g (14 oz/2⅔ cups) cooked meat
2 small Lebanese (short) cucumbers
30 g (1 oz) bundle of harusame noodles
3 teaspoons dried wakame pieces
80 ml (2½ fl oz/⅓ cup) Japanese rice vinegar
1 tablespoon mirin
1½ teaspoons Japanese soy sauce
1 teaspoon finely grated ginger and its juice
1 teaspoon caster (superfine) sugar
1 small handful mitsuba or flat-leaf (Italian) parsley,
   shredded
3 shiso leaves, finely shredded
1 spring onion (scallion), thinly sliced
12 rice paper wrappers, 20 cm (8 in) in diameter

dipping sauce
½ teaspoon dashi granules
125 ml (4 fl oz/½ cup) Japanese rice vinegar
1 tablespoon caster (superfine) sugar
1 small red chilli, seeded and very thinly sliced

makes 12

Remove the meat from the crabs, cover and refrigerate. Halve the cucumbers lengthways, scoop out the seeds with a teaspoon, then slice the flesh thinly. Sprinkle liberally with salt and allow to rest for 30 minutes. Rinse and drain well, squeezing out any excess moisture, then chill. Meanwhile, soak the harusame in warm water for 10 minutes to soften. Drain well and cut into short lengths using scissors. Soak the wakame in cold water for 5 minutes, then drain well and slice. Add to the cucumber and chill.

To make a dressing, combine the rice vinegar, mirin, soy sauce, grated ginger and juice, sugar and a pinch of salt and stir until the sugar dissolves. Put the crabmeat, cucumber, noodles, wakame, mitsuba, shiso and spring onion in a bowl, then pour over the dressing, mixing well. Chill well.

To make the dipping sauce, combine the dashi granules, rice vinegar, sugar, chilli and 60 ml (2 fl oz/¼ cup) water in a small saucepan and bring to the boil. Cook for 4–5 minutes, or until slightly syrupy. Cool to room temperature.

When you are ready to make the rolls, dip the rice paper wrappers in a bowl of cold water to soften. Lay them flat on a tea towel and put 2 tablespoons of the crab mixture near the end closest to you, then roll up, tucking the ends in about halfway. Serve immediately with the dipping sauce.

hint: You can make these rolls a few hours in advance. Store the rolls between layers of plastic wrap and refrigerate until you are ready to serve.

Tataki, a method of preparing beef by briefly searing it, is considered by the Japanese to be a form of sashimi. Here the beef is served with fresh, peppery salad leaves and a gingery soy dressing.

beef tataki salad

2 large handfuls mizuna or baby rocket (arugula)

2 x 250 g (9 oz) eye fillet steaks (cut from the middle part of the fillet)

ground white pepper

1 tablespoon vegetable oil

1 spring onion (scallion), thinly sliced on the diagonal

dressing

2 tablespoons Japanese soy sauce

1 tablespoon Japanese rice vinegar

1 tablespoon sake

½ teaspoon Japanese mustard

1 garlic glove, crushed

1 teaspoon finely grated ginger and its juice

1 teaspoon caster (superfine) sugar

½ teaspoon sesame oil

1 tablespoon vegetable oil

serves 4 as a starter

Cut the mizuna into 3 cm (1 ¼ in) lengths, rinse and drain, then chill in the refrigerator.

Season the steaks with salt and white pepper. Heat the oil in a heavy-based frying pan, add the steaks and sear on each side for about 2 minutes, or until well browned, then plunge immediately into a bowl of iced water to stop the cooking process. Remove the steaks and pat dry with paper towels. Set aside.

To make the dressing, put the soy sauce, vinegar, sake, mustard, garlic, ginger and juice, sugar, sesame and vegetable oils in a small bowl and whisk well to combine.

Slice the beef thinly across the grain, then arrange the slices, slightly overlapping each slice, on a plate. Pile the chilled mizuna on top of the beef, pour over the dressing, then sprinkle with the spring onion.

hint: Make this a light summery main course for two by serving it with some rice or noodles.

You can be as creative as you like with the coating on these fried prawns. Try sesame seeds, flaked almonds or *panko*, Japanese breadcrumbs, which are larger than traditional breadcrumbs and make a very light and crisp coating for deep-fried foods.

crispy prawns with japanese tartare

20 raw king prawns (shrimp), peeled and deveined,
    tails intact
plain (all-purpose) flour, to coat
ground white pepper
1 egg, lightly beaten with a dash of cold water
sesame seeds, flaked almonds or Japanese
    breadcrumbs, to coat
vegetable oil, for deep-frying
60 ml (2 fl oz/¼ cup) sesame oil
lemon wedges, to serve

japanese tartare
175 g (6 oz) Japanese mayonnaise
1½ tablespoons Japanese cucumber pickles
    or dill pickles, finely chopped
1 tablespoon Japanese rice vinegar
1 spring onion (scallion), white part only, finely
    chopped
1 small handful mitsuba or flat-leaf (Italian) parsley,
    chopped
1 garlic clove, crushed
ground white pepper

serves 4 as a starter

To make the Japanese tartare, put the mayonnaise, pickles, vinegar, spring onion, mitsuba and garlic in a small bowl and stir to combine. Season to taste with salt and white pepper. Chill until ready to serve.

Lightly score the belly, or underside, of the prawns. Turn them over and, starting from the tail end, press down gently at intervals along the length of the prawn—this helps to break the connective tissue, preventing the prawns from curling up too much when cooked.

Season the flour with salt and white pepper. Lightly coat the prawns in the flour, avoiding their tails, then dip into the egg, allowing any excess to drip off. Coat with your choice of sesame seeds, almonds or breadcrumbs, pressing to help them adhere. Refrigerate while you heat the oil.

Fill a deep-fat fryer or large heavy-based saucepan one-third full with vegetable oil and add the sesame oil. Heat the oil to 180°C (350°F), or until a cube of bread dropped into the oil browns in 15 seconds. Deep-fry the prawns in batches for 2 minutes, or until golden. Drain on paper towels and serve immediately, accompanied by the tartare and lemon wedges.

hint: Experiment with other crispy coatings for the prawns. Try chopped nuts, dried noodles such as harusame or soba cut into short lengths, or even finely chopped seaweed, such as wakame. Instead of prawns, try squid or calamari. Oysters are also a favourite, deep-fried in Japanese breadcrumbs.

This free-form sushi allows you to experiment with non-Japanese fillings—the suggestions given below will get you started. The only two essential Japanese ingredients you'll need are sushi rice and nori.

sushi hand rolls

sushi rice

550 g (1 lb 4 oz/2½ cups) Japanese short-grain white rice

5 x 5 cm (2 x 2 in) piece of kombu, wiped with a damp cloth (optional)

2 tablespoons sake (optional)

80 ml (2½ fl oz/⅓ cup) Japanese rice vinegar

1½ tablespoons caster (superfine) sugar

½ teaspoon salt

6 sheets of nori, cut in half

mediterranean fillings

basil leaves, prosciutto, asparagus, cooked or raw tuna, aïoli, salami, mozzarella or bocconcini, capers, artichokes, olives, sun-dried tomatoes

mexican fillings

raw tuna or salmon, avocado, coriander (cilantro) leaves, finely sliced red or green chilli, spring onion (scallion), cucumber, tomato, pickles, jalapeños

chinese fillings

barbecued duck, barbecued pork, spring onion (scallion), hoisin sauce, capsicum (pepper), cucumber

makes 12

To make the sushi rice, rinse the rice several times in cold water, or until the water runs clear, then drain in a colander for 1 hour.

Put the rice in a saucepan with 750 ml (26 fl oz/ 3 cups) cold water and, if using them, the kombu and sake. Bring to the boil, then discard the kombu. Cover with a tight-fitting lid, reduce the heat to low and simmer for 15 minutes. Turn off the heat but leave the pan on the hotplate. Remove the lid and place a clean tea towel across the top to absorb excess moisture, then put the lid on and rest for 15 minutes. Alternatively, cook the rice in a rice cooker, following the manufacturer's instructions.

Tip the rice into a wide, shallow non-metallic container and spread it out. Combine the vinegar, sugar and salt, stirring until the sugar has dissolved, then sprinkle over the warm rice. Using quick, short strokes mix the rice and liquid together with a damp wooden rice paddle or thin wooden spoon, being careful not to mush the rice. (Traditionally the rice is cooled with a hand-held fan while mixing the liquid into the rice.)

When cooled, cover with a clean, damp tea towel. For best results, use the rice immediately and do not refrigerate it. However, if you are not making your sushi within 1–2 hours, the rice must be refrigerated or bacteria may develop.

Choose your selection of fillings, and cut the larger ingredients into small strips or lengths. Place the filling ingredients on a platter and the sushi rice in a bowl. Hold a piece of nori in your hand, put a small amount of rice into the centre of the nori, then top with a few of the filler ingredients. Roll up and enjoy with accompaniments of your choice.

hint: Fill some small bowls with water and mix in a little rice vinegar. Dip your fingers into the water before assembling the hand rolls, as this prevents the rice from sticking to your fingers.

Although I love the smooth creaminess of plain tofu, it's also great when cooked with other ingredients—its soft, porous texture absorbs flavours so easily. These tofu fries have a spicy, crisp shell and a soft, fluffy centre.

spicy tofu fries

2 x 500 g (1 lb 2 oz) blocks cotton (firm) tofu
2 teaspoons Japanese chilli sesame oil
60 ml (2 fl oz/¼ cup) Japanese soy sauce
3 teaspoons finely grated ginger
4 garlic cloves, crushed
2 tablespoons white miso
vegetable oil, for deep-frying
175 g (6 oz/1 cup) potato starch
1½–2 tablespoons seven-spice mix
ground white pepper
seven-spice mix, to serve (optional)

serves 6–8 as a snack

Wrap each block of tofu in a clean tea towel and put in separate large bowls. Put a plate on the top of each block, sit a heavy tin on top and weigh down for 2 hours to extract any excess moisture. Unwrap and pat dry. Cut each block into 1.5 cm (⅝ in) thick slices, then cut the slices into fingers, 1.5–2 cm (⅝–¾ in) wide.

To make a marinade for the tofu, combine the chilli sesame oil, soy sauce, ginger, garlic and miso in a bowl and stir until smooth. Pour half into a large, shallow non-metallic dish. Add the tofu, then pour over the remaining marinade, carefully shaking the dish to help coat the tofu fingers. Cover tightly and refrigerate overnight to allow the flavours to absorb into the tofu, shaking the dish occasionally to help disperse the marinade.

When ready to cook, fill a deep-fat fryer or deep heavy-based saucepan one-third full with oil and heat to 180°C (350°F), or until a cube of bread dropped into the oil browns in 15 seconds. Combine the potato starch and seven-spice mix and season with a little salt and white pepper. Gently scrape any excess marinade from the tofu fingers, then dip them into the seasoned flour and shake off any excess. Cook in four batches for 5–6 minutes each batch, or until golden. Drain well on paper towels, sprinkle with salt, to taste, and serve immediately with extra seven-spice mix, if desired.

hint: To make a dip for the tofu fries, combine some Japanese mayonnaise with a little lemon juice and some freshly chopped mitsuba or parsley. Sprinkle with black sesame seeds and serve with the fries. They are also good with sweet chilli sauce.

yakitori plate

yakitori sauce

500 g (1 lb 2 oz) chicken wings, cut into 3 pieces
   at the joints
375 ml (13 fl oz/1½ cups) mirin
250 ml (9 fl oz/1 cup) sake
375 ml (13 fl oz/1½ cups) Japanese soy sauce
55 g (2 oz/¼ cup) caster (superfine) sugar
3 teaspoons kuzu starch rocks or arrowroot

chicken

4 small bamboo skewers, soaked in water for 1 hour
1 large chicken thigh fillet, cut into 12 even pieces
2 baby leeks or thick spring onions (scallions), white
   part only, cut into 8 short lengths

asparagus

4 small bamboo skewers, soaked in water for 1 hour
4 streaky bacon rashers, cut in half
8 x 5 cm (2 in) lengths of asparagus

enoki

4 small bamboo skewers, soaked in water for 1 hour
4 small bundles of trimmed enoki, 2 cm (¾ in)
   in diameter
4 streaky bacon rashers

shiitake

4 small bamboo skewers, soaked in water for 1 hour
12 small shiitake mushrooms or 12 halves of larger
   shiitake mushrooms, stems discarded
sea salt flakes

makes 16 skewers (4 of each type)

To make the yakitori sauce, preheat the griller
(broiler) to high. Cook the chicken wings, turning
occasionally, for 15 minutes, or until dark golden
and starting to blacken slightly. Remove and set
aside. Pour the mirin and sake into a saucepan
over high heat and bring to the boil. Add the soy
sauce and sugar and stir until the sugar has
dissolved. Add the wings and bring the liquid to the
boil, then reduce to a simmer for 30 minutes.

Remove the pan from the heat and allow to cool
for 30 minutes. Strain the sauce (you can serve the
chicken wings as a snack). Pour a little of the
sauce into a small dish and add the kuzu. Crush
the rocks and stir into the liquid until dissolved, then
return to the pan. Put the pan over high heat and
stir until the mixture boils and becomes thick and
glossy—about 20 minutes. Remove from the heat
and allow to cool before using.

To make the chicken skewers, thread 3 pieces of
chicken and 2 pieces of leek onto each skewer,
starting with a piece of chicken and alternating with
leek. Pour a little of the sauce into a small dish for
basting and reserve some for serving. Heat a griller
to high and cook the skewers, turning regularly, for
3–4 minutes, then baste with the sauce. Cook on
each side for a further 1–2 minutes, basting again,
until well glazed and the chicken is cooked through.
Serve with a drizzle of the sauce.

To make the asparagus skewers, wrap a piece of
bacon around each piece of asparagus. Thread
2 pieces onto each skewer. Put under a hot griller
for 2 minutes on each side, then brush with a little
sauce. Grill for a further 30 seconds on each side.

To make the enoki skewers, wrap a piece of bacon
around a bundle of mushrooms, so their heads are
poking out, and skewer to secure. Put under a hot
griller for 2 minutes on each side, then brush with a
little sauce. Grill for 30 seconds on each side.

To make the shiitake skewers, thread 3 shiitake
onto each skewer. Sprinkle with sea salt, put under
a hot griller for 2 minutes on each side, or until
cooked. You can also baste these lightly with
yakitori sauce during the last minute of cooking.

dirty ninja saketini

½ small Lebanese (short) cucumber
5 x 2 cm (2 x ¾ in) piece of kombu, wiped with a
    damp cloth
1 tablespoon Japanese rice vinegar
1 teaspoon caster (superfine) sugar
125 ml (4 fl oz/½ cup) well-chilled drinking sake
125 ml (4 fl oz/½ cup) well-chilled vodka

serves 4

Halve the cucumber lengthways, scoop out the
seeds with a teaspoon, and thinly slice the flesh.
Sprinkle liberally with salt and sit for 10 minutes.
Rinse off and squeeze out any excess moisture with
your hands. To make a cucumber vinegar, combine
the kombu, rice vinegar and sugar in a small bowl,
then add the cucumber and combine well. Allow to
sit for at least 1 hour. To serve, place a small mound
of cucumber in the base of four well-chilled large
martini glasses. Combine the sake and vodka and
divide between the glasses. Add a small splash of
the cucumber vinegar and serve.

ginger mizuwari

2 teaspoons fresh ginger juice
125 ml (4 fl oz/½ cup) Japanese malt whisky
4 long, thin, diagonal slices of ginger
chilled water

serves 4

Combine the ginger juice and whisky and divide
between four glasses filled with ice cubes. Add a
long slice of fresh ginger to each, then top with as
much chilled water as you like. Stir and serve.

bloody wasabi oyster shooter

½ teaspoon wasabi paste
1 tablespoon fresh lime juice
small pinch of dashi granules
small pinch of caster (superfine) sugar
125 ml (4 fl oz/½ cup) chilled tomato juice
60 ml (2 fl oz/¼ cup) shochu or drinking sake
4 freshly shucked small oysters

serves 4

Whisk together the wasabi, lime juice, dashi granules
and sugar until the dashi has dissolved, then mix in
the tomato juice and shochu. Place an oyster in
the base of four 60 ml (2 fl oz/¼ cup) chilled shot
glasses, then pour over the tomato mixture and
serve immediately.

green tea chuhai

2 teaspoons Japanese green tea powder
125 ml (4 fl oz/½ cup) shochu or drinking sake
4 long strips of lemon or lime zest, tied into knots
chilled lemonade

serves 4

Put the green tea powder in a small bowl and
whisk in 1½ tablespoons boiling water until smooth,
then allow to cool. Strain into a bowl and combine
with the shochu. Divide between four tall glasses
filled with some ice and add the lemon or lime
knots. Top up with the lemonade.

From left: Green tea chuhai, Dirty ninja saketini, Ginger mizuwari.

Gyoza, or dumplings, are traditionally pan-fried, but this deep-fried version goes best with the slightly sweet and tangy plum dipping sauce.

gyoza with pickled plum sauce

200 g (7 oz) packet gyoza wrappers (30 wrappers)
vegetable oil, for deep-frying

plum dipping sauce
8 Japanese pickled plums
185 ml (6 fl oz/¾ cup) plum wine
60 ml (2 fl oz/¼ cup) plum vinegar or Japanese
    rice vinegar
115 g (4 oz/½ cup) caster (superfine) sugar
2 teaspoons finely grated ginger and its juice

filling
200 g (7 oz) Chinese cabbage, stems removed,
    finely chopped
200 g (7 oz) minced (ground) pork
3 teaspoons finely grated ginger
3 garlic cloves, crushed
1½ tablespoons Japanese soy sauce
2 teaspoons sake
2 teaspoons mirin
¼ teaspoon ground white pepper
2 spring onions (scallions), finely chopped

makes 30

To make the plum dipping sauce, prick the plums all over with a fork, then soak them in several changes of cold water for 2 hours to remove the excess salt. Drain, pat dry, then remove the seeds and purée the flesh in a small food processor or using a stick blender. Put the puréed flesh in a small saucepan with the remaining ingredients and 185 ml (6 fl oz/¾ cup) water. Stir over high heat to dissolve the sugar, bring to the boil and cook for 15–20 minutes, or until the sauce is slightly syrupy. Cool to room temperature.

To make the filling, put the cabbage in a colander, sprinkle with salt and stand for 30 minutes. Squeeze well, then mix with the rest of the filling ingredients.

Lay a wrapper in the palm of your hand and put 2 teaspoons of the filling in the middle. Lightly dampen the edge of the wrapper with a little water, then fold the edges together to form a semicircle, pressing firmly to enclose the filling. Lightly dampen the curved edge of the wrapper, then overlap around the edge to form pleats. Put each gyoza on a tray lined with plastic wrap. Repeat with the remaining wrappers and filling. Refrigerate until ready to cook.

Fill a deep-fat fryer or deep heavy-based saucepan one-third full with vegetable oil and heat to 180°C (350°F), or until a cube of bread dropped into the oil browns in 15 seconds. Cook the gyoza in three batches for 3–4 minutes, or until golden and bubbly and the filling is cooked through. Drain well on paper towels and serve with the dipping sauce.

hint: If you prefer to pan-fry the gyoza, heat a little vegetable oil in a large non-stick frying pan over medium–high heat. Put the gyoza, flat-side down, in the pan in a single layer, leaving a little space between each. Cook them in batches for 2 minutes, or until the bottoms are crisp and golden. Combine 125 ml (4 fl oz/½ cup) boiling water with 2 teaspoons each of vegetable oil and sesame oil and add to the pan. Cover, reduce the heat to low and cook for about 10 minutes. Remove the lid, increase the heat to high and cook until the liquid has evaporated, making sure the dumplings don't catch on the base of the pan and burn. Remove from the pan and sit them flat on paper towels to drain. Serve with a simple dipping sauce of equal parts soy sauce and rice vinegar.

This appetizer is great for those new to the sushi experience because, unlike regular sushi or sashimi, the fish is not raw. This sushi is quite large and is best eaten with a knife and fork rather than with your fingers.

smoked salmon sushi

sushi rice

175 g (6 oz/¾ cup) Japanese
    short-grain white rice
5 x 2 cm (2 x ¾ in) piece of kombu, wiped with a
    damp cloth (optional)
3 teapoons sake (optional)
1½ tablespoons Japanese rice vinegar
2 teaspoons caster (superfine) sugar
¼ teaspoon salt

2 Lebanese (short) cucumbers, unpeeled, halved
    lengthways, seeded and cut into 1 cm (½ in) dice
3 tablespoons Japanese mayonnaise
1 tablespoon thinly sliced chives, plus extra
    to garnish
½ teaspoon lemon juice
100 g (3½ oz) smoked salmon slices
½ teaspoon wasabi paste
2 tablespoons salmon roe or flying fish roe

serves 4 as a starter

To make the sushi rice, rinse the rice several times in cold water, or until the water runs clear, then drain in a colander for 1 hour.

Put the rice in a saucepan with 250 ml (9 fl oz/ 1 cup) cold water and, if using them, the kombu and sake. Bring to the boil, then discard the kombu. Cover with a tight-fitting lid, reduce the heat to low and simmer for 15 minutes. Turn off the heat but leave the pan on the hotplate. Remove the lid and place a clean tea towel across the top to absorb excess moisture, then put the lid on and rest for 15 minutes. Alternatively, cook the rice in a rice cooker, following the manufacturer's instructions.

Tip the rice into a wide, shallow non-metallic container and spread it out. Combine the vinegar, sugar and salt, stirring until the sugar has dissolved, then sprinkle over the warm rice. Using quick, short strokes mix the rice and liquid together with a damp wooden rice paddle or thin wooden spoon, being careful not to mush the rice. (Traditionally the rice is cooled with a hand-held fan while mixing the liquid into the rice.) When cooled, cover with a clean, damp tea towel. For best results, use the rice immediately and do not refrigerate it. However, if you are not making your sushi within 1–2 hours, the rice must be refrigerated or bacteria may develop.

Combine the cucumber, mayonnaise, chives and lemon juice in a small bowl and season.

Using all the rice, wet your hands and then mould the rice into four large ovals. Line up the four ovals along the bench in front of you, with one of the short sides towards the end of the bench. Lightly press your hand down onto the rice to slightly flatten the ovals. Using a tablespoon, make a slight indentation on the top of each oval—this hollow is where the cucumber salad will sit.

Trim the edges of the salmon to neaten. Using your finger, smear one side of each salmon slice with a little wasabi, then neatly wrap it around the outside edge of each rice oval, wasabi-side in. The salmon should come just up to, or a little above, the rim of the rice. Top each oval with one-quarter of the cucumber mixture, then add one-quarter of the salmon roe. Garnish with a few snipped chives.

hint: These could also be made as bite-sized versions, perfect for serving at cocktail parties.

To make Japanese-style fried chicken, the chicken is marinated in soy sauce, garlic and ginger, then dusted with potato starch and quickly fried, leaving it meltingly tender and with the crispiest of coatings.

crispy nori chicken

1 kg (2 lb 4 oz) chicken thigh cutlets, skin on
60 ml (2 fl oz/¼ cup) Japanese soy sauce
60 ml (2 fl oz/¼ cup) mirin
1 tablespoon sake
2 teaspoons finely grated ginger and its juice
3 garlic cloves, crushed
vegetable oil, for deep-frying
80 ml (2½ fl oz/⅓ cup) sesame oil (optional)
85 g (3 oz/½ cup) potato starch
2 tablespoons nori flakes
⅛ teaspoon sansho pepper
lemon wedges, to serve

serves 6–8 as a snack

Remove the bone from the chicken cutlets and cut the chicken into 4 cm (1½ in) squares. Combine the soy sauce, mirin, sake, ginger and juice, and garlic in a non-metallic bowl and add the chicken. Stir to coat, cover with plastic wrap, and marinate in the refrigerator for 1 hour only (the flavour becomes too strong if left for longer than this).

Fill a deep-fat fryer or large saucepan one-third full with vegetable oil and add the sesame oil, if using. Heat to 180°C (350°F), or until a cube of bread dropped into the oil browns in 15 seconds.

Combine the potato starch with the nori flakes, sansho pepper and a large pinch of salt. Drain the chicken well, discarding the marinade. Lightly coat the chicken with the potato starch mixture and shake off any excess.

Deep-fry in batches for 6–7 minutes, or until golden and crisp and the chicken is just cooked through. Drain well on paper towels and sprinkle with salt. Serve with lemon wedges.

hint: Try this recipe with white fish fillets, prawns (shrimp) or squid, but you won't need to marinate or cook them for as long.

The Japanese have taken the gourmet pizza to new heights—there is even a website devoted to the topic—and most pizza joints have an incredible, if not bizarre, array of topping combinations.

blue cheese, prawn and shimeji pizza

20 g (¾ oz) butter

1 large onion, thinly sliced

60 ml (2 fl oz/¼ cup) mirin

1 ready-made 250 g (9 oz) pizza base, about 26 cm (10½ in) in diameter

1 tablespoon white miso

12 raw king prawns (shrimp), peeled and deveined

1 garlic clove, crushed

2 teaspoons olive oil

70 g (2½ oz/¾ cup) shimeji mushrooms, pulled apart into small clumps

150 g (5½ oz/1 cup) crumbled mild blue cheese

serves 4–6 as a snack

Melt the butter in a saucepan over low heat, add the onion and mirin and cook, stirring regularly, for 1 hour, or until deep golden and caramelized. Remove from the heat.

Preheat the oven to 220°C (425°F/Gas 7). Spread the miso on the pizza base, then top with the onion. Toss the prawns with the garlic and olive oil and evenly distribute over the onion. Scatter the shimeji and blue cheese over the top and place in the preheated oven for 25 minutes, or until the base is crisp and the top is golden and bubbling.

Remove from the oven, slice and serve. Make it a meal by serving with a green salad and Chilled tofu with roasted tomatoes (page 31).

japanese-style cabbage rolls

3 dried shiitake mushrooms

1 tablespoon vegetable oil

1 teaspoon sesame oil

5 spring onions (scallions), thinly sliced

2–3 teaspoons finely grated ginger

2 garlic cloves, crushed

½ teaspoon sansho pepper

400 g (14 oz) minced (ground) pork

115 g (4 oz/½ cup) Japanese short-grain rice

4 tablespoons finely chopped mitsuba or
    flat-leaf (Italian) parsley

ground white pepper

1 large whole Chinese cabbage (about 1.6 kg/
    3 lb 8 oz)

1 teaspoon dashi granules

2 tablespoons Japanese soy sauce

2 tablespoons sake

2 tablespoons mirin

60 ml (2 fl oz/¼ cup) Japanese rice vinegar

80 ml (2½ fl oz/⅓ cup) vegetable oil

Japanese mustard, to serve (optional)

dipping sauce

60 ml (2 fl oz/¼ cup) Japanese soy sauce

1½ tablespoons Japanese rice vinegar

2 teaspoons mirin

2 teaspoons caster (superfine) sugar

½ teaspoon chilli sesame oil

makes 16

Soak the shiitake in boiling water for 30 minutes to soften. Drain, discard the stems and finely chop the caps. Set aside. Heat the vegetable and sesame oils in a small saucepan, add the spring onions, ginger, garlic and sansho and cook, stirring over medium heat, for about 1½ minutes, or until the spring onions have softened and the mixture is fragrant. Allow to cool.

Combine the pork with the cooled spring onion mixture, the reserved shiitake, and the rice and mitsuba. Season well with salt and white pepper and mix thoroughly. Set aside.

Bring a large saucepan of water to the boil. Trim 5 cm (2 in) from the white base of the cabbage. Put the remaining cabbage in the water and boil for 5 minutes. As the leaves start to come away from the cabbage, gently pull them away from the head and allow to wilt completely. Remove to a colander to drain. Continue until you have removed all the large leaves and only a small head is left, then add it to the other leaves. Take 750 ml (26 fl oz/3 cups) of the cooking liquid and, while still hot, add the dashi granules and stir until dissolved. Add the soy sauce, sake, mirin, rice vinegar and oil and set aside.

Lay one of the larger cabbage leaves, vein-side down, on the work surface. Put a heaped tablespoon of pork mixture at the base and roll up the leaf, tucking in the sides halfway. Continue in this way, using the larger leaves—you should have about 16 rolls.

Line a large heavy-based saucepan or flameproof casserole dish with three-quarters of the remaining cabbage leaves, then snugly put the rolls in a single layer on top, seam-side down. Cover with more cabbage leaves. Pour over enough of the reserved cooking liquid mixture to just cover the leaves, then place over high heat and bring to the boil. Cover, reduce to a simmer, and cook for 1 hour, or until the pork and rice are cooked through.

To make the dipping sauce, combine all ingredients in a bowl and stir until the sugar has dissolved.

Remove the rolls with a slotted spoon and serve with the sauce and the Japanese mustard on the side, if using. If you are not serving straight away, cool slightly, then place the rolls in a ceramic dish, pour over the cooking liquid, cover and refrigerate. Reheat gently in a large saucepan.

I first tried these at a popular Japanese fast-food chain where they serve all kinds of burgers with rice 'buns' instead of bread.

teriyaki chicken riceburger

800 g (1 lb 12 oz/4 cups) freshly cooked Japanese short-grain rice, slightly cooled—you will need 325 g (11½ oz/1½ cups) raw rice

2 teaspoons sesame seeds

1½ tablespoons vegetable oil

60 ml (2 fl oz/¼ cup) Japanese soy sauce

2 tablespoons mirin

2 tablespoons sake

1½ tablespoons caster (superfine) sugar

4 x 150 g (5½ oz) chicken thigh fillets, skin on (or buy thigh cutlets and remove the bone)

1 handful mizuna leaves

2 small Lebanese (short) cucumbers, thinly sliced into ribbons (using a vegetable peeler)

Japanese mayonnaise, to serve

serves 4

Spread the warm rice into a lightly oiled 40 x 25 cm (16 x 10 in) tin, then press down and smooth over the surface so that it is flat and even. Dampen your hands to do this, as this will prevent the rice from sticking to your hands. Sprinkle over the sesame seeds and press down to adhere. Allow to cool to room temperature. Using a 9 cm (3½ in) round cookie cutter, stamp out rounds of rice and carefully set aside. Dip the cutter in hot water between each stamping so the rice doesn't stick.

Put a large non-stick frying pan over medium–high heat, brush with a little of the vegetable oil and, working in two batches, cook the rice rounds on both sides for 5 minutes each side, or until lightly golden and a little crispy. Drain on paper towels, then place on a baking tray lined with baking paper and keep warm in a low oven.

Combine the soy sauce, mirin, sake and sugar. Put the remaining oil in a large frying pan (do not use a non-stick pan this time or the sauce won't glaze properly) and heat over medium–high heat. Add the chicken, skin-side down, and cook for 4–5 minutes, or until the skin is golden. Turn over and cook for 3–4 minutes, or until lightly golden and the chicken is almost cooked through. Remove from the pan.

Discard any excess fat from the pan and pour in the soy sauce mixture, increase the heat to high and bring to the boil. Cook for 1 minute, or until the sauce is slightly glazy. Return the chicken to the pan and turn to coat well in the glaze. Take the pan off the heat.

Place a rice round on a serving plate as your 'bun' base and top with mizuna, a few cucumber ribbons, a piece of chicken, skin-side up, and a dollop of the mayonnaise. Top with a rice 'lid', sesame-side up. Repeat with the remaining ingredients to make four burgers. Serve immediately.

hint: If you don't have time to make the rice 'buns', use lightly toasted bread rolls, or simply serve the chicken and salad with cooked rice.

bowl food

Comforting and cleansing, this soup is packed with vitamins and minerals and tastes way too good to be as healthy as it is.

mushroom and wakame broth

5 dried shiitake mushrooms

5 x 20 cm (2 x 8 in) piece of kombu, wiped with a damp cloth, cut into strips

3 tablespoons dried wakame pieces

1 tablespoon vegetable oil

½ teaspoon sesame oil

1 onion, very finely chopped

1 celery stalk, very finely chopped

1 garlic clove, crushed

60 ml (2 fl oz/¼ cup) mirin

300 g (10½ oz/6 cups) shiitake mushrooms, stems discarded, caps sliced

150 g (5½ oz/1⅔ cups) shimeji mushrooms, pulled apart

150 g (5½ oz/2 cups) whole baby oyster mushrooms, or sliced if larger

2 tablespoons tamari

100 g (3½ oz/1⅓ cups) enoki mushrooms, ends trimmed, pulled apart

1 teaspoon finely grated ginger and its juice

seven-spice mix, to serve (optional)

serves 4–6 as a light meal

Put the dried shiitake and kombu in a large saucepan with 2 litres (70 fl oz/8 cups) cold water. Bring to the boil over high heat, reduce to a simmer and cook for 5 minutes, then discard the kombu. Increase the heat and bring to the boil for another 15 minutes, then turn off the heat and allow to sit for 10 minutes to allow the mushroom flavour to infuse. Remove the shiitake with a slotted spoon and, when cool enough to handle, remove and discard the stems, thinly slice the caps and return them to the stock.

Put the wakame in a bowl and pour in enough cold water so it is just covered. Soak for 5 minutes, then drain well and set aside.

Heat the vegetable and sesame oils in a frying pan over medium–high heat, add the onion and celery and cook for 10 minutes, or until the onion is lightly golden. Add the garlic and mirin and cook for a further minute. Add the fresh shiitake and a pinch of salt and cook for 3–4 minutes, or until softened. Add the shimeji and oyster mushrooms and cook for 2 minutes.

Add the cooked mushrooms to the pan filled with the stock, then pour in the tamari. Bring to the boil, cook for 2 minutes, then remove the pan from the heat and stir in the drained wakame, enoki and the ginger and juice. Ladle into bowls and sprinkle with some seven-spice mix, if desired.

hint: Add some cooked soba noodles for a more substantial meal.

This light soup has a wonderful fresh colour and taste. Here it is served warm, although it also makes a refreshing chilled soup for summer. If you can't find *edamame*, green soya beans in their pods, try broad (fava) beans, but be sure to slip them out of their skins after cooking.

edamame and asparagus soup with mizuna pesto

650 g (1 lb 7 oz) fresh or frozen soya beans in
  the pod
20 g (¾ oz) butter
2 teaspoons soya bean oil or olive oil
1 bay leaf
1 onion, chopped
1 celery stalk, chopped
250 g (9 oz) all-purpose potatoes, such as desiree,
  peeled and cut into 1 cm (½ in) dice
2 tablespoons mirin
2 teaspoons dashi granules, dissolved in 1 litre
  (35 fl oz/4 cups) hot water
250 g (9 oz) thin asparagus, chopped

mizuna pesto

2 handfuls mizuna or rocket (arugula) leaves
1 handful mitsuba or flat-leaf (Italian) parsley,
  chopped
40 g (1½ oz/¼ cup) toasted whole almonds,
  chopped
¼ teaspoon finely chopped lemon zest
1 garlic clove, chopped
¼ teaspoon salt
80 ml (2½ fl oz/⅓ cup) soya bean oil or olive oil
25 g (1 oz/¼ cup) grated Parmesan cheese

serves 4–6 as a starter

Bring a large saucepan of water to the boil, add the soya beans, allow to come to the boil again and cook for 2–3 minutes if using frozen soya beans, or 4–5 minutes if using fresh. Drain and leave until cool enough to handle, then remove the beans from the pods. You should have about 200 g (7 oz/2 cups) of beans. Set 25 g (1 oz/¼ cup) of beans aside for garnish.

Meanwhile, to make the mizuna pesto, put the mizuna, mitsuba, almonds, lemon zest, garlic, salt and oil in a blender and process until smooth. Stir in the Parmesan. Set the pesto aside.

Put the butter, soya bean oil and bay leaf in a large saucepan over medium heat. Add the onion and celery and cook until softened but not browned—about 6 minutes—then add the potato and cook for a further minute. Add the mirin and bring to the boil. Pour in the dashi, increase the heat to high, bring to the boil again and cook for 6 minutes. Add the soya beans and asparagus and cook for 5 minutes, or until everything is very tender.

Remove from the heat, discard the bay leaf and blend until as smooth as possible using a stick blender, or wait until the mixture has cooled slightly and carefully process in batches in an upright blender. Strain through a fine sieve, scraping and pressing down on the mixture with the back of a soup ladle to extract all the liquid. You should have about 1.25 litres (44 fl oz/5 cups). Season to taste and heat gently before serving, topped with a dollop of the pesto and a few of the reserved soya beans.

hint: Add a little extra oil to any leftover pesto and stir it through pasta.

Based on a traditional Japanese dish of seaweed and shellfish dressed in vinegar, this fine noodle salad makes a lovely starter or light meal. The fresh flavours of the sea are brought to life by a slightly sweet, zippy vinaigrette.

chilled prawn, cucumber and noodle salad

12 cooked king prawns (shrimp)

2 Lebanese (short) cucumbers

1 tablespoon dried wakame pieces

100 g (3½ oz) somen noodles

3 spring onions (scallions), thinly sliced on the diagonal

seven-spice mix (optional)

dressing

½ teaspoon dashi granules

125 ml (4 fl oz/½ cup) Japanese rice vinegar

60 ml (2 fl oz/¼ cup) mirin

1 teaspoon Japanese soy sauce

2 teaspoons very finely grated ginger and its juice

pinch of sugar

½ teaspoon sesame oil

serves 4 as a starter

Peel and devein the prawns, cut them in half lengthways, then refrigerate until ready to use. Halve the cucumbers lengthways, scoop out the seeds with a teaspoon, then slice very thinly on a slight diagonal. Put in a colander, sprinkle with salt and rest for 10 minutes, then rinse and squeeze out as much water as you can. Chill in the refrigerator.

Soak the wakame in cold water for 5 minutes—it should be rehydrated and glossy but not mushy. Drain, then chill.

Meanwhile, to make the dressing, mix the dashi granules with 1 tablespoon hot water and stir until dissolved. Add the rice vinegar, mirin, soy sauce, grated ginger and juice, the sugar and sesame oil. Stir to combine, then chill.

Bring a large saucepan of water to the boil, then reduce to a simmer. Add the somen and cook for 2 minutes, or until tender, then quickly drain and rinse under cold running water until the noodles are completely cooled.

Combine the noodles, prawns, cucumber, wakame and half the spring onions with the dressing and toss well. Serve immediately, garnished with the remaining spring onions and sprinkled with the seven-spice mix, if desired.

The Japanese have such a fondness for corn potage that it is available in packet form—just add water or milk. While this version may take a little more time, the results are well worth the effort. Surprisingly rich, this soup is best served in small bowls as a starter.

corn potage

5 x 10 cm (2 x 4 in) piece of kombu, wiped with
    a damp cloth, cut into strips

4 cobs sweet corn

20 g (¾ oz) butter

1 teaspoon sesame oil

1 leek, thinly sliced

1 celery stalk, finely chopped

1 garlic clove, crushed

1 teaspoon finely grated ginger

60 ml (2 fl oz/¼ cup) mirin

125 ml (4 fl oz/½ cup) cream

ground white pepper

sesame oil, to serve

Japanese soy sauce, to serve (optional)

nori flakes or thinly sliced spring onion (scallion),
    to garnish

serves 4–6 as a starter

To make a stock, put the kombu and 1 litre (35 fl oz/4 cups) cold water in a large saucepan. Slowly bring to the boil, cook for 30 seconds, then remove the kombu. Cut the kernels from the corn cobs, then add both the corn kernels and the cobs to the pan and return to the boil. Reduce to a simmer and cook for 10 minutes, then remove from the heat and set the saucepan aside.

In a clean saucepan, add the butter and sesame oil and melt over medium heat. Add the leek and cook, stirring regularly, for 6 minutes, or until lightly golden. Add the celery, garlic and ginger and cook for 1 minute, or until fragrant.

Remove the corn cobs, but not the kernels, from the stock and discard. Add the corn stock and the mirin to the leek mixture and bring to the boil over high heat, then reduce to a simmer and cook for 15 minutes. Remove from the heat and, using a stick blender, purée the soup until as smooth as possible, or wait until cooled slightly and carefully process in batches in an upright blender.

Push the mixture through a fine sieve into a clean saucepan, pressing down on the solids to help extract more liquid. Discard the solids. Stir in the cream and heat gently over low heat—do not allow to boil. Season to taste with salt and white pepper. Serve in small bowls dotted with a little sesame oil and soy sauce, if using, and sprinkle with nori flakes or spring onion. Great with Nori, sesame and parmesan pastries (page 19).

hint: Add a little more cream to the soup if you find it is too thick.

Here's a wonderful Japanese version of soul-warming chicken soup. It's light, fresh and flavoursome and very good for you.

chicken and vegetable broth

350 g (12 oz) daikon, peeled, cut into
   5 cm (2 in) lengths
1 large carrot, peeled, cut into 5 cm (2 in) lengths
1 celery stalk, cut into 5 cm (2 in) lengths
1 leek, cut into 5 cm (2 in) lengths
80 g (2¾ oz) snow peas (mangetout), trimmed
50 g (1¾ oz/¼ cup) drained, sliced tinned bamboo
   shoots
1.5 kg (3 lb 5 oz) whole chicken
8 spring onions (scallions), bruised
110 g (3¾ oz/1 cup) sliced ginger
8 garlic cloves, bruised
5 x 20 cm (2 x 8 in) piece of kombu, wiped with a
   damp cloth
2 teaspoons dashi granules
4 small dried shiitake mushrooms
ground white pepper
4 long strips of lemon zest, tied into knots
Japanese chilli sesame oil (optional)

serves 4–6 as a light meal

Finely julienne the daikon, carrot, celery and leek, using either the coarse-tooth blade on a Japanese mandolin or a sharp knife. Cut the snow peas and bamboo shoots into matchsticks.

Rinse the cavity of the chicken, then put it into a large, deep saucepan, breast-side down. Add the spring onions, ginger, garlic, kombu, dashi, shiitake and 3 litres (105 fl oz/12 cups) cold water. Bring to the boil over high heat, then reduce to a simmer and cook for 5 minutes. Remove the kombu. Continue to simmer for 12 minutes, skimming any foam off the surface, then carefully turn the chicken over and simmer for a further 15–20 minutes, or until the thigh juices run clear when pierced.

Remove the shiitake and chicken from the broth, tipping any liquid in the cavity of the chicken back into the pan. Cover the chicken with foil and set aside to cool slightly. Strain the stock into a clean saucepan. Remove and discard the shiitake stems, slice the caps and return them to the pan with the stock. Bring the stock to a boil, reduce the heat and simmer for 10 minutes. Add the julienned and matchstick vegetables and cook for 8–10 minutes, or until just tender. Season to taste with salt and white pepper and remove from the heat.

Remove the breasts and legs from the chicken. Discard the skin and cut the meat into short, neat strips.

Place a little breast and leg meat into the base of each soup bowl, along with a knot of lemon zest, then ladle over the broth and vegetables. Pass around some chilli sesame oil for drizzling, if desired. Serve with chopsticks and a spoon.

hint: As a variation, add 200 g (7 oz) silken firm tofu, cut into dice, to each bowl before ladling over the broth.

Burdock has a wonderful earthy flavour —to me, it tastes like a cross between Jerusalem artichokes and bamboo shoots. Combined with prosciutto and sage, it develops a rich, savoury accent. If you can't find fresh burdock, it is available frozen in Asian grocery stores, peeled and ready for cooking.

burdock cream soup with crispy prosciutto and sage

800 g (1 lb 12 oz) fresh burdock root

1 tablespoon Japanese rice vinegar

1½ tablespoons olive oil

a few drops of sesame oil

1 large onion, finely chopped

1 celery stalk, finely chopped

1 carrot, finely chopped

2 garlic cloves, finely chopped

3 teaspoons finely chopped sage

2 tablespoons mirin

700 g (1 lb 9 oz) floury potatoes, such as russet (Idaho), peeled and diced

1.25 litres (44 fl oz/5 cups) chicken broth or chicken stock

10 g (¼ oz) butter

12 whole large sage leaves

6 long slices prosciutto

250 ml (9 fl oz/1 cup) cream

serves 4–6 as a starter

Lightly scrape the burdock with a knife to remove its thin brown skin, then dice and put in a bowl of water with the rice vinegar. This maintains the pale colour of the burdock and also helps to remove any bitterness.

Put 1 tablespoon of the olive oil and the sesame oil in a large saucepan over medium heat. Add the onion, celery and carrot and cook until softened and lightly golden. Add the garlic, sage and mirin and cook for 1 minute. Drain the burdock and add it to the pan, along with the potato and stock. Bring to the boil over high heat, then reduce to a simmer and cook for 1 hour, or until the burdock is tender.

Remove from the heat and, using a stick blender, purée the soup, or wait until cooled slightly and carefully process in batches in a food processor or an upright blender. Strain twice through a fine sieve into a clean saucepan to remove any tough fibrous matter, pushing down with a wooden spoon to extract all the liquid.

Put the butter and remaining oil in a frying pan over medium–high heat, then add the sage leaves and cook, stirring occasionally, for a few minutes, or until crispy and aromatic. Remove and drain on paper towels. Add the prosciutto and cook for about 3 minutes, or until crispy. Drain on paper towels, then break into small pieces.

Stir the cream into the soup and place on a gentle heat to warm through. Season to taste, then ladle into bowls. Garnish with a little prosciutto and some fried sage leaves. Serve with crusty bread.

Green tea soba noodles, made with buckwheat flour and finely ground green tea, look and taste spectacular when combined with bright, fresh vegetables, crispy bacon and a velvety sesame soy dressing.

green tea noodle salad

200 g (7 oz) green tea soba noodles, cut in half

3 teaspoons dried hijiki or wakame pieces

2 teaspoons vegetable oil

4 bacon rashers, thinly sliced

150 g (5½ oz/1 cup) cherry tomatoes,
   cut in half

70 g (2½ oz/1½ cups) baby English spinach leaves,
   rinsed and drained well

1 ripe avocado, cut into 1.5 cm (⅝ in) cubes

sesame seeds, to serve

sesame soy dressing

2 tablespoons Japanese soy sauce

60 ml (2 fl oz/¼ cup) Japanese rice vinegar

1½ tablespoons mirin

2½ teaspoons sesame oil

2 garlic cloves, crushed

1 teaspoon caster (superfine) sugar

1½ teaspoons finely grated ginger and its juice

1 tablespoon toasted sesame seeds

serves 4 as a starter

Bring a large saucepan of salted water to the boil over high heat, then gradually lower the soba noodles into the water. Stir so the noodles don't stick together. Add 250 ml (9 fl oz/1 cup) cold water and return to the boil. Repeat this step another two or three times, or until the noodles are tender. This method helps to cook this delicate noodle more evenly. The noodles should be *al dente*—there should be no hard core in the centre, but they should not be completely soft all the way through either.

Drain, then rinse well under cold running water, rubbing together lightly with your hands to remove any excess starch. Put the noodles in a bowl filled with water and ice cubes until they are completely chilled. Drain well.

Meanwhile, put the hijiki in a bowl and cover with cold water. Lightly rub the pieces between your fingers to break up and to loosen any dirt, then lift the hijiki out of the water and put in a clean bowl filled with cold water. Soak for 8 minutes, then drain and pour boiling water over them. Drain well. If using wakame, put it in a bowl and pour in enough cold water to just cover. Soak for 5 minutes, then drain well and set aside.

To make the sesame soy dressing, combine all the ingredients in a bowl and set aside.

Heat the oil in a frying pan, add the bacon and cook over medium–high heat for 4–5 minutes, or until crispy. Drain on paper towels and set aside.

Combine the noodles with two-thirds of the dressing, then fold in the hijiki or wakame, bacon, tomatoes, spinach and avocado. Place in a mound in a bowl and drizzle over the remaining dressing. Sprinkle with extra sesame seeds and serve immediately.

This hearty, filling dish is similar to a Middle Eastern chickpea soup. You can, in fact, substitute chickpeas if preferred, but the cooking time will be shorter. Prepare this ahead of time as soya beans need to be soaked overnight.

soya bean and cumin soup

500 g (1 lb 2 oz/2⅔ cups) dried soya beans

5 x 10 cm (2 x 4 in) piece of kombu, wiped with a damp cloth

2 tablespoons soya bean oil or olive oil

1 large onion, chopped

1 bay leaf

1 carrot, chopped

2 celery stalks, chopped

4 garlic cloves, crushed

2 teaspoons ground cumin

1 teaspoon ground cinnamon

1 teaspoon seven-spice mix

large pinch of bicarbonate of soda (baking soda)

1 tablespoon dashi granules

1½ tablespoons soya bean oil or extra virgin olive oil, extra

1½ tablespoons lemon juice

2 tablespoons finely chopped mitsuba or flat-leaf (Italian) parsley

serves 6 as a starter, or 4 as a main

Soak the soya beans and kombu overnight in cold water, then drain, discarding the kombu. Put the soya beans in a large saucepan filled with water, bring to the boil and cook for 5 minutes, then drain and rinse well.

Heat the soya bean oil in a large saucepan and add the onion and bay leaf and cook over medium heat for 5 minutes, or until lightly golden. Add the carrot and celery and cook for 10 minutes, or until softened and slightly caramelized. Add the garlic, cumin, cinnamon and seven-spice mix and cook for 30 seconds, or until fragrant. Add the soya beans, bicarbonate of soda and 3.5 litres (122 fl oz/ 14 cups) cold water (don't add salt or the beans won't soften properly). Bring to the boil over high heat, then reduce to a simmer and cook for about 4 hours, or until the beans are very soft, skimming occasionally to remove any foam from the surface.

Add the dashi and stir to dissolve. Take the pan off the heat, remove the bay leaf and purée the soup using a stick blender, or wait until cooled slightly and process in a food processor until smooth. Season to taste. The soup will thicken on standing so you may need to add a little extra water if reheating.

Combine the extra soya bean oil with the lemon juice and mitsuba. Ladle the soup into bowls and drizzle the mitsuba and oil mixture over the top.

hint: The time it takes to cook soya beans depends on the age of the beans and storage conditions, so it may take more or less than the times given.

This chunky soup is really a meal in a bowl—a warming, aromatic broth brimming with tender, fresh seafood and vegetables.

spicy miso seafood hotpot

250 g (9 oz) baby clams (vongole)

12 black mussels

12 raw medium prawns (shrimp)

12 large scallops without roe

400 g (14 oz) salmon fillet

2 small squid tubes (about 100 g/3½ oz each), cleaned

1 tablespoon vegetable oil

1 teaspoon sesame oil

2 leeks, thinly sliced

1–2 small red chillies, seeded and finely chopped

1 bay leaf

5 garlic cloves, finely chopped

1 tablespoon very finely chopped ginger

80 ml (2½ fl oz/⅓ cup) sake

60 ml (2 fl oz/¼ cup) mirin

2 teaspoons dashi granules, dissolved in 2 litres (70 fl oz/8 cups) hot water

5 x 10 cm (2 x 4 in) piece of kombu, wiped with a damp cloth

1 tablespoon Japanese soy sauce

12 small new potatoes, peeled

200 g (7 oz/2½ cups) sliced Chinese cabbage

3 tablespoons white or red miso

1 log of kamaboko, about 160 g (5½ oz), cut into 12 even slices

1 small handful mitsuba or flat-leaf (Italian) parsley

lemon wedges, to serve

Japanese chilli sesame oil (optional)

serves 6 as a main

Soak the clams in several changes of cold water for about 2 hours to rid them of sand. Drain well. Scrub the mussels, remove their beards, and discard any mussels that are cracked or open. Peel and devein the prawns, leaving the tails intact. Remove the muscle from the scallops. Remove any bones from the salmon and cut into 3 cm (1¼ in) pieces. Cut the squid into 1 cm (½ in) thick rings. Put all the seafood in the refrigerator, in separate groups.

Heat the vegetable and sesame oils in a very large saucepan over medium heat, then add the leek, chilli and bay leaf and cook for 10 minutes, or until the leek is golden. Add the garlic and ginger and cook for 1 minute.

Increase the heat to high and add the sake, mirin, clams and mussels and cook, shaking the pan, for 4–6 minutes. When the shells open, remove from the pan and set aside (still in their shells). Discard any shells that remain closed.

Add the dashi mixture, kombu, soy sauce and potatoes to the pan. Bring to the boil, remove the kombu, and cook for 15 minutes, or until the potato is quite tender. Skim any foam from the surface. Reduce to a simmer, add the cabbage and cook for 4 minutes, or until the cabbage is wilted. Add the prawns, scallops, salmon and squid, bring to a simmer again and cook for 2–3 minutes, or until everything is just cooked through. Remove the solids from the broth with a slotted spoon and divide the ingredients equally between six deep, wide bowls. Cover with foil to keep warm.

Increase the heat to high. Mix a little of the hot broth into the miso to form a paste, then add to the pan with the kamaboko, the clams and mussels (and any juices) and heat for 1–2 minutes. Divide the solids between the bowls, then ladle over the remaining soup. Scatter with a few mitsuba leaves and serve with lemon wedges and chilli sesame oil for drizzling over, if desired.

Sweet potatoes are popular in Japan, and in the cooler months street vendors roast them over hot coals and serve them topped with a knob of butter, which melts into the soft smoky flesh—the aroma is irresistible. Not quite so aromatic but just as delicious are these delicate gnocchi—the pancetta and butter adding rich, nutty flavours.

sweet potato gnocchi with pickled ginger brown butter

2 x 600 g (1 lb 5 oz) orange sweet potatoes

2 egg yolks

2 tablespoons finely grated Parmesan cheese, plus extra to serve

300 g (10½ oz/2½ cups) plain (all-purpose) flour

2 teaspoons vegetable oil

150 g (5½ oz) pancetta, finely diced

125 g (4½ oz) butter

60 g (2¼ oz/¼ cup) pickled ginger, rinsed, squeezed dry, finely shredded

3 garlic cloves, crushed

90 g (3¼ oz/2 cups) chopped mizuna, baby rocket (arugula) or spinach leaves

serves 6 as starter, or 4 as main

Preheat the oven to 200°C (400°F/Gas 6). Prick the sweet potatoes all over, then cook for 2 hours, or until very tender. Set aside until cool enough to handle, then peel and mash well. Put the mashed sweet potato in a clean tea towel and twist and squeeze out any excess moisture.

Mix the mashed sweet potato with the egg yolks and Parmesan, then gradually stir in the flour. When it forms a soft dough, remove to a lightly floured work bench and knead gently for a minute to just bring it together—add a little extra flour if needed. You should have a soft, pliable dough that is slightly damp but not sticky. Do not overwork the dough or it will toughen.

Heat the oil in a frying pan and cook the pancetta over medium–high heat for 4–5 minutes, or until frizzled and crispy. Drain on paper towels.

Bring a large saucepan of salted water to the boil. Divide the dough into quarters and roll each into smooth 1.5 cm (⅝ in) thick ropes, then cut each rope into 2 cm (¾ in) lengths with a sharp knife. You should end up with about 85 gnocchi.

Cook the gnocchi in four batches for 1–2 minutes, or until they rise to the surface. Lift them out with a slotted spoon, transfer to a bowl and toss with 1–2 teaspoons olive oil.

Meanwhile, put the butter and pickled ginger in a saucepan over medium heat and cook, stirring regularly, for 3–4 minutes, or until the butter foams, then turns golden brown and has a nutty aroma. Stir in the garlic and remove the pan from the heat immediately to make sure the garlic doesn't burn. Add to the gnocchi, along with the mizuna and pancetta and toss to combine. Season to taste with a little salt and freshly ground black pepper and serve with extra Parmesan to sprinkle over.

Fans of garlicky vongole, or baby clams, need look no further. This aromatic version uses sake, ginger and dashi granules. Dashi is made from dried bonito, a type of tuna, and its addition helps boost the overall seafood flavour. Slurp them one by one from the shells, or serve over freshly cooked udon noodles or linguine for pasta vongole, Japanese style.

sake-steamed clams with garlic and chilli

1 kg (2 lb 4 oz) baby clams (vongole)

80 ml (2½ fl oz/⅓ cup) vegetable oil

1 teaspoon sesame oil

6 garlic cloves, thinly sliced lengthways

2 small red chillies, seeded and thinly sliced

1 small leek, very thinly sliced

60 ml (2 fl oz/¼ cup) drinking sake

ground white pepper

1 teaspoon finely chopped ginger

large pinch of dashi granules

15 g (½ oz) butter

3 tablespoons chopped mitsuba or flat-leaf (Italian)
   parsley

lemon wedges, to serve

450 g (1 lb) udon noodles, freshly cooked (optional)

serves 6 as a starter, or 4 as a main

Soak the clams in several changes of cold water for about 2 hours to rid them of sand. Drain well.

Heat the vegetable and sesame oils in a large saucepan over low heat, add the garlic and chilli and cook, stirring regularly, until the garlic is golden and crisp (do not allow the garlic to burn or it will become bitter). Remove with a slotted spoon and drain on paper towels.

Add the leek to the pan and cook for 5 minutes, or until softened. Increase the heat to high and add the sake and clams, a pinch each of salt and white pepper, the ginger and dashi granules. Cover and cook for 5 minutes, shaking the pan occasionally, until all the clams are open. Discard any that remain closed. Stir in the garlic and chilli, the butter and mitsuba and serve immediately with lemon wedges on the side for squeezing over. If you like, serve with udon noodles.

As Japanese rice is quite glutinous you will notice that this recipe calls for a little more liquid than a regular risotto. If you can't find all the fantastic Japanese mushrooms used here, simply substitute with funghi of your choice.

japanese mushroom risotto

4 dried shiitake mushrooms

5 x 5 cm (2 x 2 in) piece of kombu, wiped with a damp cloth

2½ tablespoons Japanese soy sauce

80 ml (2½ fl oz/⅓ cup) mirin

40 g (1½ oz) butter

100 g (3½ oz/2 cups) shiitake mushrooms, stems discarded, caps sliced

150 g (5½ oz/1⅔ cups) shimeji mushrooms, pulled apart

150 g (5½ oz/2 cups) oyster mushrooms, sliced

1 tablespoon vegetable oil

1 teaspoon sesame oil

1 onion, finely chopped

1 celery stalk, finely chopped

2 garlic cloves, crushed

2 teaspoons grated ginger

450 g (1 lb/2 cups) Japanese short-grain rice

100 g (3½ oz/1⅓ cups) enoki mushrooms, ends trimmed, pulled apart

2 handfuls mitsuba or flat-leaf (Italian) parsley, finely chopped

25 g (1 oz/1 bunch) chives, chopped

shaved Parmesan cheese, to serve

serves 6 as a starter, or 4 as a main

Put the dried shiitake and kombu in a saucepan with 1.875 litres (65 fl oz/7½ cups) water and bring to the boil over high heat. Turn off the heat and sit for 15 minutes. Discard the kombu. Discard the mushroom stems, thinly slice the caps and set aside. Bring the stock back to the boil, then reduce to a simmer and add the soy sauce and mirin.

Melt half of the butter in a saucepan over medium-high heat, then add the fresh shiitake, shimeji and oyster mushrooms and a pinch of salt and cook for 8–10 minutes, or until the mushrooms are wilted and any liquid has cooked off. Set aside.

Melt the remaining butter with the vegetable and sesame oils in a large saucepan over medium–high heat. Add the onion and celery and cook for about 5 minutes, or until the onion is lightly golden. Add the garlic and ginger and cook for 30 seconds, or until aromatic.

Add the rice and stir to coat in the butter and onion mixture. Cook, stirring, for 2 minutes, or until the rice is slightly translucent. Gradually stir in 125 ml (4 fl oz/½ cup) of the simmering liquid, stirring until it has almost been absorbed, then continue to add the remaining stock, 125 ml (4 fl oz/½ cup) at a time, stirring constantly until the stock has been absorbed. This should take about 25 minutes. With the last 125 ml (4 fl oz/½ cup) of liquid, add the cooked mushrooms, the sliced shiitake, and the enoki, stirring to heat through.

Remove from the heat, scatter over the mitsuba and chives and season, to taste. Serve immediately with Parmesan. Great with Green salad with Japanese dressing (page 142).

Confusingly, this recipe is called 'yakisoba'—in fact, it does not use soba noodles but a soft Chinese-style egg noodle, sold in Japanese stores as yakisoba. If you can't find them, use thin hokkien (egg) or udon noodles.

yakisoba with prawns

4 dried shiitake mushrooms

1 kg (2 lb 4 oz) raw medium prawns (shrimp), peeled and deveined

3 garlic cloves, finely chopped

1½ teaspoons finely chopped ginger

3 rashers streaky bacon, cut into 3 cm (1¼ in) lengths

1 tablespoon vegetable oil

1 teaspoon sesame oil

1 carrot, thinly julienned

1 small green capsicum (pepper), cut into thin strips

200 g (7 oz) Chinese cabbage, cut into 3 cm (1¼ in) squares

100 g (3½ oz/½ cup) drained, sliced tinned bamboo shoots, thinly sliced lengthways

6 spring onions (scallions), cut into 3 cm (1¼ in) lengths

500 g (1 lb 2 oz) yakisoba noodles, separated

1 tablespoon thinly sliced pickled ginger

lemon wedges, to serve (optional)

yakisoba sauce

2 tablespoons Japanese soy sauce

60 ml (2 fl oz/¼ cup) Worcestershire sauce

1 tablespoon Japanese rice vinegar

1½ tablespoons sake

1 tablespoon tomato sauce (ketchup)

1 tablespoon oyster sauce

3 teaspoons black sugar or dark brown sugar

½ teaspoon dashi granules

serves 4–6 as a main

Soak the shiitake in hot water for 30 minutes. Drain, reserving 2 tablespoons of the liquid, discard the mushroom stems and slice the caps. Combine the prawns with half the garlic and half the ginger.

To make the yakisoba sauce, combine all the sauce ingredients in a bowl, along with the reserved mushroom soaking liquid, and set aside.

Heat a wok over medium–high heat, add the bacon and stir-fry for 2–3 minutes, or until lightly browned. Remove and set aside. Combine the vegetable and sesame oils, add half to the wok and increase the heat to high. Add the prawns and stir-fry for 1–2 minutes, or until they just turn pink. Remove and add to the bacon.

Add a little more of the combined oils to the wok, then add the carrot, capsicum, cabbage, bamboo shoots and shiitake and stir-fry for 4–5 minutes. Add the spring onions and remaining garlic and ginger and stir-fry for a further minute. Remove from the wok and set aside.

Add the remaining oil to the wok and stir-fry the noodles for 1 minute. Add the vegetables, sauce and pickled ginger and stir-fry for 3 minutes, then add the prawns and bacon and cook for a further 2–3 minutes, or until the prawns are cooked through and the sauce glazes the noodles. Serve with lemon wedges to squeeze over if desired.

hint: This dish is also good sprinkled with nori flakes or bonito flakes.

This brothy stew is light on the stomach but big on flavour and texture.

chicken and eight vegetable stew

200 g (7 oz) fresh burdock root

1 teaspoon Japanese rice vinegar

200 g (7 oz) fresh lotus root

1 tablespoon vegetable oil

2 teaspoons sesame oil

2 kg (4 lb 8 oz) whole chicken, cut into
    10 even-sized pieces, lightly seasoned

200 g (7 oz) taro, peeled and cut into
    3 cm (1¼ in) cubes

2 carrots, thickly sliced

100 g (3½ oz/2 cups) small shiitake mushrooms,
    stems discarded

100 g (3½ oz/½ cup) drained, sliced tinned
    bamboo shoots

2 teaspoons dashi granules, dissolved in
    1 litre (35 fl oz/4 cups) hot water

125 ml (4 fl oz/½ cup) Japanese soy sauce

1½ tablespoons caster (superfine) sugar

80 ml (2½ fl oz/⅓ cup) mirin

100 g (3½ oz) snow peas (mangetout), trimmed

3 spring onions (scallions), cut into 4 cm (1½ in)
    lengths on the diagonal

serves 6–8 as a main

Gently scrape the thin skin from the burdock root, then rinse. Starting at the thin end and using a small sharp knife, shave off pieces as if you are sharpening a pencil with a knife. Put the shavings in a small bowl of vinegared water and set aside. This not only helps to remove any bitterness but also prevents the burdock from turning brown. Peel the lotus, then cut into 5 mm (¼ in) slices and put into a bowl of cold water.

Heat the vegetable and sesame oils in a large saucepan over medium–high heat. Add the chicken pieces in two batches and cook until golden—about 10 minutes per batch. Set aside.

Add the taro and carrot to the saucepan and cook, stirring regularly, for 2 minutes, then add the well-drained burdock and lotus and cook for 2 minutes, or until lightly golden. Add the shiitake and bamboo shoots and cook for 2 minutes.

Add the dashi, soy sauce, sugar, mirin and chicken pieces (along with any juices) and bring to the boil. Reduce to a simmer and cook for 12–15 minutes, or until the chicken is just cooked through and the vegetables are tender. The breast pieces may cook more quickly than the others—if so, remove from the pan and return to the heat just before serving. Add the snow peas and spring onions and cook for 1 minute, or until tender. Serve with rice.

hint: If fresh burdock and lotus are not available, you can find them in the freezer compartment of Japanese or Asian grocery stores.

This dish, originally Chinese, uses soba noodles. Soba, or buckwheat, noodles are made from wheat flour and ground buckwheat seeds, which gives them their distinctive brown colouring and slightly nutty flavour.

soba with sautéed pork, eggplant and chilli

60 ml (2 fl oz/¼ cup) vegetable oil

1 teaspoon sesame oil

3 long, slender eggplants (aubergines), sliced 1.5 cm (⅝ in) thick

3 garlic cloves, crushed

1½ teaspoons finely grated ginger

6 spring onions (scallions), sliced on the diagonal, white and green parts kept separate

600 g (1 lb 5 oz) minced (ground) pork

2 tablespoons chilli bean sauce

1 tablespoon tomato paste (purée)

½ teaspoon dashi granules

2 tablespoons mirin

1 tablespoon Japanese soy sauce

1 teaspoon soft brown sugar

250 g (9 oz) soba noodles

extra sesame oil, to drizzle (optional)

serves 4 as a main

Put 2 tablespoons of the vegetable oil and the sesame oil in a wok over medium–high heat (do not use a non-stick wok for this recipe). Add the eggplant slices and cook, stir-frying until golden on both sides, for about 4–5 minutes. Drain on paper towels and set aside.

Add the remaining vegetable oil to the wok, then add the garlic, ginger and the white part of the spring onions and cook for 30 seconds, then remove and set aside. Add the pork and brown well all over, using a fork to break up any lumps—this should take 6–8 minutes.

Add the chilli bean sauce, tomato paste, dashi granules, mirin, soy sauce, sugar and 250 ml (9 fl oz/1 cup) water to the wok, along with the spring onion and garlic mixture. Allow to come to the boil, then reduce to a simmer and cook for 5 minutes. Add the eggplant and most of the spring onion greens, reserving some for garnish, and cook for 3 minutes, or until the eggplant is cooked through. Increase the heat to high and cook until most of the liquid has evaporated and the mixture is slightly glazy—about 4–5 minutes.

Bring a large saucepan of salted water to the boil over high heat. Add the soba, stirring so they don't stick together, and return to the boil. Add 125 ml (4 fl oz/½ cup) cold water and return to the boil. Repeat this procedure twice more, or until the noodles are *al dente*. Drain, then rinse well under cold running water, rubbing the noodles lightly between your hands to remove any excess starch.

Pile the noodles into a 'nest' in the centre of the plate. Top with the meat and eggplant sauce and garnish with the reserved spring onions. Serve with sesame oil for drizzling over, if desired.

hint: Brands of chilli bean sauce differ in flavour and heat, so use with caution. One of my favourites is the Chinese brand, Pun Chun.

This simple recipe is based on a Japanese home-style dish, *niku jaga*, which traditionally uses beef. Lamb is rarely used in Japanese cuisine but in this dish it really works.

lamb shank and potato stew

700 g (1 lb 9 oz) all-purpose potatoes, such as desiree, peeled

2 tablespoons vegetable oil

1 large onion, cut into thin wedges

6 large lamb shanks (about 1.5 kg/3 lb 5 oz)

ground white pepper

1 teaspoon sesame oil

2 teaspoons dashi granules

125 ml (4 fl oz/½ cup) Japanese beer, such as Kirin, Asahi or Sapporo

60 ml (2 fl oz/¼ cup) Japanese soy sauce

125 ml (4 fl oz/½ cup) sake

2 tablespoons black sugar or dark brown sugar

60 g (2¼ oz/⅓ cup) drained, sliced tinned bamboo shoots

serves 4–6 as a main

Cut the potatoes into 3–4 cm (1¼–1½ in) chunks, then bevel the edges by running a sharp knife or vegetable peeler along the sharp edges so the shape is softened and slightly rounded. This also prevents them from breaking up too much during cooking. Soak in cold water for 30 minutes, then drain well and thoroughly pat dry with paper towels.

Heat 2 teaspoons of the vegetable oil in a large saucepan over medium–high heat. Add the onion and cook, stirring occasionally, for 5 minutes, or until lightly browned. Remove and set aside. Add another 2 teaspoons of oil to the pan, add the potatoes and toss well to coat. Cook, shaking the pan regularly, for about 7 minutes, or until the potatoes are lightly golden, then set aside.

Season the lamb shanks with a little salt and white pepper. Add the remaining vegetable oil and the sesame oil to the pan, then cook the shanks in batches for 5 minutes, or until they are well browned on all sides.

Return the onions to the pan, along with the dashi granules, beer, soy sauce, sake, sugar and 1 litre (35 fl oz/4 cups) cold water and stir to combine. Increase the heat and bring to the boil, removing any foam that rises to the surface. Cover, reduce to a simmer and cook for 1¼ hours.

Add the potatoes and bamboo shoots and cook, uncovered, continuing to remove any foam, for a further 45 minutes, or until both the potato and meat are very tender but not falling apart.

Serve in bowls with a little of the broth poured over. Alternatively, for a richer dish, remove the lamb shanks and potato from the pan, cover and set aside. Increase the heat to high and boil the liquid for 20–25 minutes to reduce slightly. Carefully return the lamb and potato to the pan and turn to coat in the sauce, then reduce the heat to low and gently heat through. Serve a shank in a shallow bowl with a few pieces of potato and spoon over the sauce. Great with a bowl of hot, lightly buttered mixed greens.

This is the Japanese version of spaghetti and meatballs. Ginger and tomato are a surprisingly great combination and make for a light, zesty sauce.

chicken meatballs in gingery tomato sauce

chicken meatballs

700 g (1 lb 9 oz) chicken thigh fillets, minced (ground)

4 spring onions (scallions), finely chopped

1 large garlic clove, crushed

1 egg

1 egg yolk

2 tablespoons sake

2 tablespoons Japanese soy sauce

60 g (2¼ oz/1 cup) Japanese breadcrumbs

ground white pepper

1 tablespoon vegetable oil

1 teaspoon sesame oil

sauce

1 tablespoon vegetable oil

1 small onion, finely chopped

1 small red chilli, seeded and finely chopped

1 garlic clove, crushed

1 tablespoon finely grated ginger and its juice

60 ml (2 fl oz/¼ cup) mirin

2 x 400 g (14 oz) tins crushed tomatoes

1 tablespoon tomato paste (purée)

¼ teaspoon dashi granules

1½ teaspoons Japanese soy sauce

½ teaspoon caster (superfine) sugar

3 tablespoons finely chopped mitsuba or flat-leaf (Italian) parsley

450 g (1 lb) udon noodles, freshly cooked, to serve

serves 4–6 as a main

To make the meatballs, put the chicken, spring onions, garlic, egg, egg yolk, sake, soy sauce and breadcrumbs in a bowl, season lightly with salt and white pepper and mix thoroughly. Cover and refrigerate until ready to use.

To make the sauce, heat the vegetable oil in a large saucepan over medium heat, then add the onion and cook, stirring regularly, for 5 minutes, or until lightly golden. Add the chilli, garlic and ginger and juice and stir for 30 seconds, or until fragrant.

Add the mirin, tomatoes, tomato paste, dashi granules, soy sauce, sugar and 250 ml (9 fl oz/ 1 cup) cold water to the pan, then increase the heat and allow to come to the boil. Reduce to a simmer and cook for 40 minutes, or until slightly thickened and pulpy. Set aside.

Form the chicken mixture into walnut-sized balls (about 1 level tablespoon for each). Heat the vegetable and sesame oils over medium–high heat in a non-stick frying pan and cook the balls in batches for 5 minutes, or until lightly golden all over.

Return the sauce to medium–high heat and add the chicken balls. When the mixture comes to the boil, reduce to a simmer and cook for 5 minutes, or until the balls are cooked through. Stir through the mitsuba or parsley and season, to taste. Serve with freshly cooked udon noodles.

Based on the French favourite, beef bourguignon, this adaptation contains fresh shiitake mushrooms, peppery sansho, dry sake and rich, earthy miso. *Bon appétit*, or, as the Japanese would say—*itadakimasu*.

beef, shiitake and red wine stew

60 ml (2 fl oz/¼ cup) vegetable oil

6 baby leeks, cut into 4 cm (1½ in) lengths

300 g (10½ oz/6 cups) shiitake mushrooms, stems discarded, caps cut in half if large

1 large onion, chopped

1 large carrot, chopped

4 streaky bacon rashers, chopped

2 tablespoons plain (all-purpose) flour

1 teaspoon sansho pepper

pinch of sea salt flakes

1 kg (2 lb 4 oz) stewing beef, cut into large cubes

3 garlic cloves, crushed

375 ml (13 fl oz/1½ cups) red wine

375 ml (13 fl oz/1½ cups) sake

2 tablespoons red miso

serves 6 as a main

Heat 1 tablespoon of the oil in a large saucepan over medium heat. Add the leeks and cook until lightly golden, then remove them to a plate and set aside. Add the shiitake and cook for a few minutes, or until softened and lightly browned, then remove to the plate with the leeks. Set the leeks and mushrooms aside until ready to use.

Add the onion, carrot and bacon to the pan and cook for 10 minutes, or until lightly browned, then remove and set aside, separate from the leeks.

Combine the flour, sansho pepper and sea salt in a large bowl. Toss with the beef to coat well.

Add a little more oil to the pan and brown the beef in batches. Remove and set aside. Add the garlic to the pan and stir for a few seconds, then add the red wine and sake and stir, scraping up any sediment stuck to the base of the pan.

Return the beef to the pan, along with the onion, carrot and bacon, the miso and 250 ml (9 fl oz/ 1 cup) water. Increase the heat to high, stir until the miso dissolves, then bring to the boil. Reduce the heat to low, cover and simmer for 1½ hours, then add the leeks and shiitake to the pan and cook, uncovered, for a further 30 minutes, or until the beef is very tender and the sauce has thickened. Serve with Mitsuba mash (page 158).

main plates

Sometimes the most simple of cooking methods can yield the best results. Japanese cooks have a fondness for steaming, which helps to retain flavours and nutrients, and keeps the food tender and moist. The subtle 'ocean flavour' of wakame brings out the natural sweetness of the fish.

steamed snapper with wakame

2 tablespoons dried wakame pieces

4 x 175 g (6 oz) snapper fillets

2 spring onions (scallions), thinly sliced on the
    diagonal

2 tablespoons drinking sake

20 g (¾ oz) butter

1 teaspoon finely grated ginger and its juice

2 teaspoons Japanese soy sauce

1 tablespoon lemon juice

¼ teaspoon sesame oil

serves 4

Put the wakame in a bowl, pour in enough cold water to just cover the wakame, and allow to soak for 2–3 minutes to soften slightly. Drain well. Put each snapper fillet on a piece of baking paper or foil approximately 30 cm (12 in) square.

Mix together the wakame and the spring onions. Drizzle the sake over the fish, then sprinkle lightly with salt. Divide the wakame mixture between the fish, then dot the butter over the top. Fold up the edges of the paper, seal tightly and put the parcels in a large bamboo steamer and cover with the lid.

Bring a wok or large saucepan filled with water to the boil. Place the steamer over the top and steam for 10–12 minutes, or until the fish is just cooked through and the flesh is opaque.

While the fish is cooking, combine the ginger and juice, soy sauce, lemon juice and sesame oil in a small serving bowl.

Place each parcel of fish on a serving platter and ask each guest to open the parcels at the table. Serve with the sauce for drizzling over.

Niçoise salad, Japanese style.

nihon niçoise

500 g (1 lb 2 oz) kipfler (fingerling) potatoes, peeled
   and sliced on the diagonal, 1 cm (½ in) thick
400 g (14 oz) fresh or frozen soya beans
   in the pod
12 cherry tomatoes, cut in half
2 spring onions (scallions), sliced on the diagonal
40 g (1½ oz/¼ cup) small black olives
1 large handful mitsuba or flat-leaf (Italian) parsley
1 tablespoon vegetable oil
4 x 175 g (6 oz) sashimi-grade tuna fillets

dressing
2 teaspoons Japanese soy sauce
2 tablespoons Japanese rice vinegar
1½ tablespoons lemon juice
1 garlic clove, crushed
80 ml (2½ fl oz/⅓ cup) extra virgin olive oil
½ teaspoon sesame oil
¼ teaspoon Japanese mustard

serves 4

Put the potatoes in a saucepan and cover with water. Place over high heat and bring to the boil. Cook for 8–10 minutes, or until tender, then drain, rinse and drain well again.

Bring a small saucepan of water to the boil, add the soya beans and cook for 2–3 minutes if frozen, and for a further 2 minutes if fresh, or until tender. Drain and refresh with cold water, then drain well again. When cool enough to handle, slip the beans from their pods.

To make the dressing, combine all the ingredients and whisk until smooth. Combine the potatoes, soya beans, cherry tomatoes, spring onions, olives and mitsuba with the dressing and toss lightly.

Heat the vegetable oil in a large heavy-based frying pan over medium–high heat. Season the tuna steaks, then cook for 1–2 minutes each side, or until cooked to your liking (ideally the inside should still be rare and pink).

Divide the salad between four plates, top with a piece of tuna and serve immediately.

The richness of the duck meat marries well with the flavours in this salad—sweet citrus, fresh daikon and slightly peppery salad leaves, all brought together with a tart but smoky soy dressing. The ponzu dressing is best made the day before to allow the flavours to develop.

crisp duck breast with orange and daikon salad

3 oranges
300 g (10½ oz) daikon
80 g (2¾ oz/2½ cups) mizuna or baby rocket
   (arugula)
4 x 175–200 g (6–7 oz) duck breast fillets
oil, for brushing
1½ tablespoons vegetable oil
1 teaspoon sesame oil
1 tablespoon drinking sake

ponzu dressing
1 teaspoon lemon juice
1 teaspoon lime juice
1 teaspoon Japanese rice vinegar
1 tablespoon Japanese soy sauce
1 teaspoon mirin
1 tablespoon sake
¼ teaspoon sugar
5 x 1 cm (2 x ½ in) piece of kombu, wiped with
   a damp cloth, julienned
1 teaspoon bonito flakes

serves 4

To make the ponzu dressing, put all the ingredients in a non-metallic bowl and stir until the sugar has dissolved. Cover with plastic wrap and refrigerate for 24 hours.

Remove the skin from the oranges and carefully remove all the pith. Segment the oranges into a bowl, then squeeze the juice from the membranes over the top. Chill.

Peel the daikon, cut in half lengthways and slice very thinly into half moons using a Japanese mandolin or a very steady hand and a sharp knife. Rinse and drain the mizuna well, then put it, along with the daikon, in the refrigerator to chill.

Lightly score through the skin and fat of the duck breasts using a sharp knife, being careful not to cut into the flesh. Season with salt, rubbing into the skin. Put a large heavy-based frying pan over medium heat and brush with a little oil. Place the seasoned duck breasts skin-side down and cook for 6 minutes to render the fat, then remove the duck from the pan.

Discard the fat, return the frying pan to the heat and increase the temperature to high. When hot, put the duck, skin-side up, in the pan and cook for 2 minutes to seal, then turn over and cook, skin-side down, for 4–5 minutes, or until crisp and golden. The flesh should still be pink inside. Remove to a plate, lightly cover and rest for a few minutes.

Strain the ponzu through muslin (cheesecloth) or a fine sieve into a bowl and add the vegetable and sesame oils and sake, along with 1 tablespoon orange juice from the bowl of oranges.

Drain the orange segments, toss together with the daikon, mizuna and the dressing and divide between four plates. Arrange the duck breasts over the top and serve immediately.

Hailing from Okinawa, and of Chinese influence, is this very rich, tender pork dish. Only small amounts are needed but it makes for a hearty meal when accompanied by rice and steamed green vegetables.

sweet simmered pork

2 teaspoons vegetable oil

½ teaspoon sesame oil

1 kg (2 lb 4 oz) boneless pork belly

150 g (5½ oz/1¼ cups) sliced ginger

2 teaspoons dashi granules

170 ml (5½ fl oz/⅔ cup) sake

60 ml (2 fl oz/¼ cup) mirin

60 ml (2 fl oz/¼ cup) Japanese rice vinegar

55 g (2 oz/⅓ cup) black sugar or dark brown sugar

60 ml (2 fl oz/¼ cup) tamari

60 ml (2 fl oz/¼ cup) Japanese soy sauce

serves 4

Heat the vegetable and sesame oils in a large heavy-based saucepan over high heat and brown the pork well on all sides. Remove from the pan and rinse the pork under hot water to remove any excess oil. Discard the fat from the pan, then return the pork to the pan and add enough cold water to cover well. Add the ginger slices and bring to the boil over high heat. Reduce to a simmer, cover and cook for 2½ hours, topping up the water if needed.

Remove the pork and 750 ml (26 fl oz/3 cups) of the cooking liquid from the pan and put into a clean saucepan, along with the dashi granules, sake, mirin, rice vinegar, sugar, tamari and soy sauce. Return to the heat and bring to the boil, then reduce to a simmer and cook, uncovered, for 1–1¼ hours, or until the pork is very tender but not falling apart. Carefully turn the pork a couple of times while it is cooking to help promote more even cooking.

Remove from the heat and allow the pork to rest in the liquid for 20 minutes, then remove and cut into slices approximately 2 cm (¾ in) thick. Serve the pork with rice and steamed green vegetables, such as bok choy (pak choi), choy sum, snow peas (mangetout) and asparagus. Spoon over some of the cooking liquid and serve. Try it with some hot Japanese mustard, *karashi*, if desired.

hint: For a more aromatic and spiced version, add a star anise and a cinnamon stick to the saucepan when you add the other flavourings during the second stage of cooking.

Salmon is one of the few fish that benefits from a flavoursome sauce—with most white-fleshed fish you can end up masking the natural flavour. The sauce used here is similar to teriyaki, but it is not as sweet because of the addition of citrus juice. This recipe is also great with tuna or swordfish.

salmon with citrus soy glaze

4 x 200 g (7 oz) salmon fillets, skin on

1 tablespoon vegetable oil

1 teaspoon sesame oil

1½ tablespoons Japanese soy sauce

60 ml (2 fl oz/¼ cup) sake

1 tablespoon mirin

1 tablespoon lemon or lime juice, or a combination of both

2 teaspoons caster (superfine) sugar

40 g (1½ oz) unsalted butter

¼ teaspoon finely grated ginger

black sesame seeds, to garnish

serves 4

Carefully check the salmon for bones, pulling any out with clean tweezers. Season lightly with salt.

Heat the vegetable and sesame oils in a large heavy-based frying pan over medium–high heat and add the salmon pieces, skin-side down. Cook for 4 minutes, or until the skin is golden. Reduce the heat to medium, turn the fish over and cook for 2–3 minutes, or until almost cooked through. Remove from the pan, cover and set aside.

Remove any excess oil from the pan, then add the soy sauce, sake, mirin, lemon juice, sugar, butter and ginger to the pan, increase the heat to high and stir to dissolve the sugar. Bring to the boil and cook for 4–5 minutes, or until the sauce is quite glazy.

Garnish with the sesame seeds and serve the sauce on the side, for drizzling over the salmon. Serve with rice and a mix of steamed green vegetables, such as asparagus, bok choy (pak choi), sugarsnap peas, snow peas (mangetout) or green soya beans.

Although the eggplant in this recipe is prepared, cooked and dressed in the traditional Japanese manner, I've strayed from tradition by pairing it with lamb, a meat introduced to Japan only in recent years. The smoky flavour of the eggplant is perfectly partnered with lamb.

lamb with grilled eggplant

6 long, slender eggplants (aubergines)

1½ tablespoons Japanese soy sauce

½ teaspoon grated ginger and its juice

1 garlic clove, crushed

⅛ teaspoon dashi granules, dissolved in
    60 ml (2 fl oz/¼ cup) hot water

pinch of caster (superfine) sugar

2 tablespoons vegetable oil

½ teaspoon sesame oil

4 x 200 g (7 oz) lamb backstraps or loin fillets

seven-spice mix, to season (optional)

shiso leaves, to garnish

serves 4

Preheat the griller (broiler) to high. Brush the eggplants with a little oil, prick them a few times with a skewer, then place under the griller and cook for about 12 minutes, turning regularly until the skin is slightly blackened and wrinkled and the flesh feels soft to the touch. Immediately remove from the heat and plunge into iced water. Leave until just cool enough to handle, then remove all blackened and blistered skin. Cut each eggplant into 4 cm (1½ in) lengths and put into a bowl.

Combine the soy sauce, ginger and juice, garlic, dashi and sugar and stir until the sugar dissolves. Pour over the eggplant and turn to coat well.

Heat the vegetable and sesame oils in a large frying pan over medium–high heat. Season the lamb with salt, pepper and the seven-spice mix, if using, and cook on each side for 3 minutes for rare, or a little longer if preferred. Remove from the pan and rest for 5 minutes. Slice off the ends on the diagonal and discard them, then slice the backstrap into two pieces, again on the diagonal and in the same direction.

Place a few shiso leaves on each plate, then arrange the eggplant and lamb on top. Drizzle over any dressing left in the bowl and serve immediately.

This dish is a little French, a little Italian and, of course, a little Japanese. I love the combination of the veal with the sweetness of the vegetables and the earthy, savoury mayonnaise. Mirin, rice vinegar and shiitake mushrooms give an extra dimension to what is basically ratatouille.

veal cutlets with japanese ratatouille and soy mayonnaise

60 ml (2 fl oz/¼ cup) vegetable oil

1 teaspoon sesame oil

1 leek, chopped

2 teaspoons grated ginger

2 garlic cloves, crushed

3 long, slender eggplants (aubergines), halved lengthways and thickly sliced

2 zucchini (courgettes), halved lengthways and thickly sliced

1 red capsicum (pepper), cut into 2 cm (¾ in) squares

100 g (3½ oz/2 cups) shiitake mushrooms, stems discarded, caps quartered

60 ml (2 fl oz/¼ cup) mirin

60 ml (2 fl oz/¼ cup) Japanese rice vinegar

185 ml (6 fl oz/¾ cup) ready-made puréed tomatoes

pinch of caster (superfine) sugar

4 x 225 g (8 oz) veal cutlets

ground white pepper

1 tablespoon finely shredded shiso or basil leaves

soy mayonnaise

2 teaspoons white miso

½ teaspoon Japanese soy sauce

1 garlic clove, crushed

125 g (4½ oz/½ cup) Japanese mayonnaise

serves 4

Heat 2 tablespoons of the combined vegetable and sesame oils in a large deep-sided frying pan over medium heat. Add the leek and cook for 5 minutes, or until lightly golden. Add the ginger and garlic and cook for a few seconds, then add the eggplant, zucchini, capsicum and shiitake and sauté for about 10 minutes, or until lightly golden. Add the mirin and cook for 1 minute, then add the vinegar, tomato purée, sugar and 60 ml (2 fl oz/ ¼ cup) water and stir to combine. Bring to the boil, then reduce to a simmer and cook for about 20 minutes, or until the vegetables are very tender but not falling apart. Season to taste.

To make the soy mayonnaise, mix the miso, soy sauce and garlic until smooth, then whisk into the mayonnaise and set aside.

Season the veal with salt and white pepper. Put the remaining oil in a large heavy-based frying pan over high heat. Add the veal and cook for 4 minutes on each side, or until cooked to your liking. Remove from the heat, cover and rest for a few minutes.

Stir the shiso through the vegetables, then divide between four plates, top with a veal cutlet and a dollop of soy mayonnaise and serve immediately.

Heat the vegetable and sesame oils in a large frying pan over low heat (don't use a non-stick pan for this recipe). Add the garlic and chilli and stir for 3 minutes, or until the garlic is evenly golden and crisp. Remove with a slotted spoon and set aside.

Increase the heat to medium–high and place the seasoned chicken, skin-side down, in the pan. Cook for 5 minutes, then turn and cook for 5 minutes on the other side, or until just cooked through. Remove and set aside.

Combine the vinegar, mirin, sugar, dashi and soy sauce with 60 ml (2 fl oz/¼ cup) water and slowly add to the pan, being careful as it may splatter. Stir to dissolve the sugar, then add the garlic and chilli and continue to stir, scraping up any cooked sediment from the base of the pan. Bring to the boil and cook for 3–5 minutes, or until slightly glazy. Return the chicken to the pan, add the shredded shiso, and turn the chicken to coat in the sauce. Remove from the heat and drizzle with any sauce left in the pan. Serve with rice and steamed greens.

hint: If you can't find shiso, try Thai basil.

This simple dish hints of Thailand, with its combination of salty, sweet, hot and sour flavours, frequently used in Thai stir-fries, dressings and dipping sauces.

caramel chicken with shiso

1 tablespoon vegetable oil

½ teaspoon sesame oil

4 garlic cloves, thinly sliced lengthways

2 small red chillies, seeded and julienned

4 x 150 g (5½ oz) chicken breast fillets,
   skin on

60 ml (2 fl oz/¼ cup) Japanese rice vinegar

60 ml (2 fl oz/¼ cup) mirin

3 tablespoons caster (superfine) sugar

⅛ teaspoon dashi granules

2 teaspoons Japanese soy sauce

4 shiso leaves, finely shredded

serves 4

In Japan, 'borrowed' words are used for many Western items, particularly food, and *hambaagaa* is one of them (read it slowly, pronouncing the 'aa' as 'ah'). Although Japanese *hambaagaas* are usually served drizzled with a mixture of soy sauce and grated daikon, which I highly recommend, I have opted here for a lovely creamy mushroom sauce.

japanese hambaagaa with mushroom sauce

300 g (10½ oz) minced (ground) pork

300 g (10½ oz) minced (ground) beef

1 small onion, finely chopped

80 g (2¾ oz/1¼ cups) Japanese breadcrumbs

2 garlic cloves, crushed

2 teaspoons finely grated ginger and its juice

1 egg, lightly beaten

60 ml (2 fl oz/¼ cup) Japanese soy sauce

60 ml (2 fl oz/¼ cup) mirin

2 teaspoons vegetable oil

½ teaspoon sesame oil

20 g (¾ oz) butter

100 g (3½ oz/2 cups) shiitake mushrooms, stems discarded, caps thinly sliced

150 g (5½ oz/1⅔ cups) shimeji mushrooms, pulled apart

200 g (7 oz/2⅔ cups) enoki mushrooms, ends trimmed, pulled apart in small clumps

¼ teaspoon dashi granules

170 ml (5½ fl oz/⅔ cup) cream

serves 4

Combine the pork, beef, onion, breadcrumbs, garlic, ginger and juice, egg, 2 tablespoons of the soy sauce and 1 tablespoon of the mirin, and season. Shape into eight equal-sized oval patties, about 2.5 cm (1 in) thick, place on a tray in a single layer, cover and refrigerate for 2 hours to allow the flavours to develop.

Heat the vegetable and sesame oils in a large non-stick frying pan over high heat and cook the patties in batches for 1–2 minutes on each side, or until browned. Reduce the heat to medium and cook for a further 3–4 minutes on each side, or until just cooked through. Remove from the pan, cover and set aside.

Add the butter to the pan, then add the shiitake, shimeji and a pinch of salt and cook for about 4 minutes, or until softened and starting to colour. Add the enoki, the remaining soy sauce and mirin, the dashi granules and cream and bring to the boil. Cook for 2 minutes, or until the sauce has thickened slightly and is of a coating consistency. Stir in any juices from the resting meat, season to taste, then add the patties and turn to coat. Cook for a further minute to heat through.

Place two patties on each plate, spoon on the mushroom sauce and serve immediately. Great with steamed greens or Green salad with Japanese dressing (page 142).

This chicken schnitzel is first marinated, then coated in breadcrumbs spiced with *shichimi togarashi*, a seven-flavour spice mix. The base of the spice mix is chilli, along with six other possible flavours—often sesame seeds, sansho pepper, shiso, mustard, nori flakes or poppy seeds. Regional variations are found at local Japanese markets.

shichimi schnitzel

4 x 175 g (6 oz) chicken thigh fillets

1½ tablespoons Japanese soy sauce

1½ tablespoons mirin

2 teaspoons finely grated ginger

3 garlic cloves, crushed

1 tablespoon seven-spice mix

60 g (2¼ oz/½ cup) plain (all-purpose) flour

½ teaspoon salt

125 g (4½ oz/2 cups) Japanese breadcrumbs

2 eggs, lightly beaten

vegetable oil, for deep-frying

125 ml (4 fl oz/½ cup) sesame oil, for deep-frying
   (optional)

chopped mitsuba or flat-leaf (Italian) parsley, to serve

lemon wedges, to serve

serves 4

Place a piece of chicken between two pieces of plastic wrap and pound with a meat mallet or the back of a heavy knife to flatten to 5 mm (¼ in) thick. Continue with the remaining chicken to make four schnitzels.

Combine the soy sauce, mirin, ginger, garlic and half the seven-spice mix in a non-metallic dish, add the chicken and turn to coat. Cover with plastic wrap and refrigerate for 1 hour.

Combine the flour with the salt in a bowl. In another bowl, combine the remaining seven-spice mix with the breadcrumbs. Lift the schnitzels out of the marinade, allowing the excess to drip off. Lightly coat the chicken in the flour, then dip into the egg and coat with the spiced breadcrumbs, pressing the breadcrumbs to help them adhere. Refrigerate for 30 minutes.

Fill a deep-fat fryer or large saucepan one-third full with vegetable oil and add the sesame oil, if using. Heat to 170°C (325°F), or until a cube of bread dropped into the oil browns in 20 seconds. Lower one or two schnitzels at a time into the oil and cook for about 5 minutes, or until golden and cooked through. Drain well on paper towels and keep warm in a very low oven while you cook the rest. Sprinkle with the mitsuba and serve immediately with lemon wedges. Great with Japanese coleslaw (page 145) and Potato salad (page 150).

hint: Make a great chicken schnitzel sandwich with some lettuce, Lebanese (short) cucumber, Japanese mayonnaise and tonkatsu sauce. Both the mayonnaise and tonkatsu sauce are available at Japanese grocery stores.

Seaweed paste is a rather unattractive black paste made from kelp, but it has a divine sweet yet salty, mellow flavour that is absolutely delicious with steak.

beef fillet steak with seaweed butter

100 g (3½ oz) unsalted butter, softened

3 teaspoons prepared seaweed paste, or to taste

1 tablespoon nori flakes

1 garlic clove, crushed

1 tablespoon vegetable oil

½ teaspoon sesame oil

4 x 200 g (7 oz) fillet steaks

1 tablespoon finely chopped chives

serves 4

Combine the softened butter with the prepared seaweed paste, nori flakes and garlic and season. Shape the butter into a small squarish log, about 4 cm (1½ in) in diameter, then wrap it in a large piece of plastic wrap. Refrigerate the butter for 20 minutes, or until firm.

When ready to start cooking the steaks, remove the butter from the fridge to soften slightly. Heat the vegetable and sesame oils in a frying pan over medium heat. Season the steaks with salt and pepper and cook for 4–5 minutes on each side for rare to medium, or until cooked to your liking.

Remove the steaks from the pan and rest for 5 minutes before topping with a couple of slices of the softened butter and a sprinkling of chives. Great with boiled new potatoes and Asian greens or a green salad.

hint: Prepared seaweed paste, *nori tsukudani*, is available in Asian grocery stores. The labels of some call it 'prepared', and others, 'seasoned', but they are the same thing. Different brands may vary in strength. The paste can be also added to sauces or soups for a boost of flavour.

Nashi, a type of Japanese pear that actually looks more like an apple, stays quite crisp when cooked this way and makes for a refreshing balance with the rich pork and mustard cream sauce. Brown nashi have a more caramel flavour than the pale green yellow-skinned variety.

pan-fried pork cutlets with nashi

2 nashi

20 g (¾ oz) butter

1 teaspoon vegetable oil

1 teaspoon sesame oil

4 x 200 g (7 oz) pork cutlets

1 small garlic clove, crushed

60 ml (2 fl oz/¼ cup) mirin

80 ml (2½ fl oz/⅓ cup) chicken stock

1 tablespoon Japanese rice vinegar

½ teaspoon Japanese mustard

170 ml (5½ fl oz/⅔ cup) cream

2 shiso leaves, finely shredded

serves 4

Trim the ends off the top and bottom of the nashi and discard them. Slice the remaining nashi into 1.5 cm (⅝ in) thick discs so that you can see the cross-section and a little star in the centre of each (you will need eight slices in total). Put the butter in a large frying pan over medium heat and fry the nashi, in batches if necessary, for about 2 minutes on each side, or until golden and slightly tender. Remove the nashi from the pan, cover to keep warm, and set aside.

Add the vegetable and sesame oils to the pan and heat over medium–high heat. Season the pork cutlets and cook on each side for 4–5 minutes, or

until just cooked through. Remove from the pan and cover to keep warm.

Add the garlic, mirin, stock and vinegar and bring to the boil, scraping up any cooked sediment on the base of the pan. Over high heat, add the mustard and cream to the pan, along with any juices from the resting pork, season to taste and bring to the boil again. Cook for 2 minutes, or until the sauce has thickened slightly.

Arrange a pork cutlet with two nashi slices on each plate and spoon over the sauce. Sprinkle the shiso over the top and serve immediately. Great with Daikon hash browns (page 153) and steamed greens or a green salad.

Although one of my absolute favourite foods is a simply seasoned, perfectly roasted chicken, I have recently become extremely fond of a different method of preparation. For this dish, you will need to start the day before, as overnight marinating allows the flavours to develop and the meat to tenderize, but it's well worth the little extra effort for succulent, flavoursome chicken.

soy roast chicken

2 kg (4 lb 8 oz) whole chicken
125 ml (4 fl oz/½ cup) Japanese soy sauce
60 ml (2 fl oz/¼ cup) mirin
60 ml (2 fl oz/¼ cup) sake
100 g (3½ oz/⅓ cup) white miso
2 tablespoons soya bean oil or vegetable oil
5 garlic cloves, bruised
80 g (2¾ oz) ginger, sliced
1 teaspoon soft brown sugar

serves 4–6

Rinse the chicken inside and out and pat dry. Put the soy sauce, mirin, sake, miso and soya bean oil in a non-metallic dish, large enough to easily fit the chicken, then mix until smooth. Add the chicken and turn to coat well in the marinade. Loosen the skin covering the breast and spoon some of the marinade under the skin and some into the cavity. Cover and refrigerate overnight, occasionally turning the chicken in the marinade.

Preheat the oven to 190°C (375°F/Gas 5). Remove the chicken from the dish, reserving the marinade, and place on a rack in a roasting tin. Stuff the cavity with the garlic and ginger and pour 500 ml (17 fl oz/2 cups) water into the base of the tin.

Sprinkle the chicken with salt, then put in the preheated oven and cook for 1–1¼ hours, or until the juices run clear when a skewer is pierced through the thickest part of the thigh. Allow to rest for 15 minutes before carving.

Meanwhile, put the reserved marinade in a small saucepan with the brown sugar and boil for about 5 minutes, or until thickened slightly. Add any resting juices from the chicken and boil until reduced again. Carve the chicken and serve with the sauce on the side. Great with Honey soy roast vegetables (page 157) and steamed Asian greens.

Marinating or preserving foods in miso has been a popular practice in Japan dating back as far as the 12th century. Although miso is used to make wonderful pickles and condiments, it also renders meat particularly tender and flavoursome. I love the slightly sweet, earthy hint that miso gives to the lamb.

lamb racks in miso

2 x 8 racks of lamb

2 tablespoons white miso

2 tablespoons red miso

2 garlic cloves, crushed

80 g (2¾ oz/1¼ cups) Japanese breadcrumbs

1 teaspoon finely chopped lemon zest

2 small handfuls mitsuba or flat-leaf (Italian) parsley,
    finely chopped

60 g (2¼ oz) butter, melted

ground white pepper

serves 4

Trim any excess fat from around the bones of the lamb racks. Combine the white and red miso with the garlic, then rub the mixture all over the meat. Place in a ceramic dish and cover tightly with plastic wrap so the miso doesn't dry out too much. Refrigerate overnight.

When ready to cook, preheat the oven to 190°C (375°F/Gas 5). To make a breadcrumb crust for the lamb, combine the breadcrumbs, lemon zest, mitsuba and melted butter in a bowl and season with a little salt and white pepper.

With a clean, damp cloth, wipe the top bones of the rack to remove any miso, as it may burn. Place the racks together so their bones interlock, then stand the racks upright in the dish (this helps to promote even cooking).

Evenly pat the breadcrumb mixture onto the outside of the rack, pressing down to adhere the crumbs. Place the rack in a roasting tin, put in the preheated oven and cook for 35 minutes, or until pink to medium–rare, or until cooked to your liking. Serve with Roast pumpkin and ginger mash (page 154) and steamed greens.

soya beans and vegetables with roasted garlic aïoli

425 g (15 oz/2¼ cups) dried soya beans

5 x 10 cm (2 x 4 in) piece of kombu, wiped with a
damp cloth

3 bay leaves

2 garlic cloves, bruised

60 ml (2 fl oz/¼ cup) soya bean oil or olive oil

40 g (1½ oz) butter

2 large onions, chopped

3 carrots, cut into 3 cm (1¼ in) lengths

2 celery stalks, cut into 3 cm (1¼ in) lengths

250 g (9 oz) daikon, cut into 2 cm (¾ in) cubes

3 long, slender eggplants (aubergines), cut into
3 cm (1¼ in) lengths

125 g (4½ oz/1½ cups) peeled and shaved fresh
burdock root (see page 188)

1½ tablespoons plain (all-purpose) flour

185 ml (6 fl oz/¾ cup) mirin

125 ml (4 fl oz/½ cup) sake

400 g (14 oz) tin crushed tomatoes

750 ml (26 fl oz/3 cups) vegetable stock, or
1¼ teaspoons dashi granules, dissolved in
750 ml (26 fl oz/3 cups) water

2 tablespoons red miso

2 tablespoons Japanese soy sauce

1 tablespoon finely chopped thyme

2 teaspoons finely grated ginger

1 teaspoon lemon zest, very finely chopped

90 g (3¼ oz/1½ cups) Japanese breadcrumbs,
seasoned

2 tablespoons finely chopped mitsuba
or flat-leaf (Italian) parsley

roasted garlic aïoli
1 head of garlic

olive oil, to drizzle

150 g (5½ oz/⅔ cup) Japanese mayonnaise

serves 6–8

Soak the soya beans and kombu overnight in cold water. Drain, discard the kombu, and put the beans in a large saucepan with 2 of the bay leaves and the garlic cloves and cover with water by 10 cm (4 in). Bring to the boil, then reduce to a simmer and cook for 2½ hours, or until tender. Rinse and drain.

Preheat the oven to 170°C (325°F/Gas 3). Heat half the oil and half the butter with the remaining bay leaf in a large, deep-sided frying pan over medium heat, add the onions and cook for 15 minutes, or until deep golden. Remove and set aside. Pour in a little more oil, if needed, then add the carrots, celery and daikon and cook, stirring occasionally, for 15 minutes, or until golden. Add to the onions. Pour in the remaining oil and add the eggplant and burdock and cook for 5 minutes, or until lightly golden, then set aside with the other vegetables.

Add the remaining butter to the pan, then add the flour and cook for 1 minute. Gradually whisk in the mirin and sake until smooth. Stir in the tomatoes, stock or dashi, miso, soy sauce, thyme, ginger and lemon zest. Bring to the boil, then reduce to a simmer for 10 minutes, or until thickened slightly.

Combine the soya beans with the vegetables and sauce. Season well. Put in a 4 litre (140 fl oz/16 cup) casserole dish and cover. Cook for 2 hours, or until the beans are tender, then uncover and sprinkle with the combined breadcrumbs and mitsuba. Cook, uncovered, for 30 minutes, or until the top is golden and crisp.

To make the aïoli, slice the top off the whole garlic head. Place in a small baking dish, drizzle with olive oil and season. Cover tightly with foil and put on a separate shelf in the oven. Cook for 25 minutes, or until the cloves are very soft. Allow to cool, then squeeze each clove from its skin and mash to a paste. Mix with the mayonnaise and season. Serve the casserole with the aïoli on the side to dollop over as desired. Great with a green salad.

Pork belly is a standard cut in Japan and other Asian countries and is now becoming increasingly popular in Western cooking. This tender meat is wonderful for roasting and the boneless, regular-shaped slabs make for shorter but more even cooking and very easy carving. Fuji apples hold together well during cooking, so are great when making a chunky-style apple sauce.

roast pork belly with fuji apple sauce

1 kg (2 lb 4 oz) boneless pork belly

1½ teaspoons sea salt flakes

vegetable oil

1 leek, sliced

1 large carrot, chopped

1 celery stalk, chopped

4 garlic cloves, bruised

2 bay leaves, crumbled

1½ tablespoons plain (all-purpose) flour

185 ml (6 fl oz/¾ cup) chicken stock

fuji apple sauce

2 Fuji apples, peeled and diced

2 teaspoons finely grated ginger and its juice

1½ tablespoons Japanese rice vinegar

80 ml (2½ fl oz/⅓ cup) mirin

pinch of sugar

serves 4

Preheat the oven to 200°C (400°F/Gas 6). Rub the pork skin with the salt flakes and a little vegetable oil. Combine the leek, carrot, celery, garlic and bay leaves and place in the centre of a roasting tin. Sit the pork on top of the vegetables and put in the oven. Pour 375 ml (13 fl oz/1½ cups) water into

the base of the tin and cook for 1 hour, or until the skin is crispy and the meat is cooked through.

While the meat is cooking, make the apple sauce. Combine the apples, ginger and juice, rice vinegar, mirin, sugar and a pinch of salt with 60 ml (2 fl oz/¼ cup) water in a small saucepan. Cook over low heat, stirring regularly so the apples don't stick to the pan, for about 40 minutes, or until the apples are very soft but not mushy—there should still be a few chunks of apple.

When the pork is cooked, remove from the heat, cover lightly with foil and rest for 10–15 minutes before carving.

While the meat is resting, tip the vegetables and juices from the roasting tin into a fine sieve over a bowl. Press down to extract as much flavour and juice as possible—you should have about 125 ml (4 fl oz/½ cup). Allow the juices to sit so the fat rises to the top. Spoon off 1½ tablespoons of fat and put into a small saucepan over medium–high heat, then stir in the flour and cook for 1 minute.

Discard any remaining fat on top of the juices, then gradually whisk the juices and the chicken stock into the flour mixture until a smooth gravy is formed. Bring to the boil and cook for 1–2 minutes, or until thickened slightly. Season to taste.

Carve the pork into thick slices and serve with gravy and apple sauce. Serve with Daikon and potato gratin (page 161), and steamed greens or Green beans with sesame miso dressing (page 146).

This slow method of cooking duck results in the crispiest of skin and a melt-in-the-mouth tender flesh. The dried zest of the yuzu, a large Japanese citrus fruit, adds an exotic flavour and aroma to the delicious savoury meat and sweet caramelized peaches.

slow-roasted duck with yuzu peaches

2.5 kg (5 lb 8 oz) whole duck

sea salt flakes

a few drops of sesame oil

1 head of garlic

80 g (2¾ oz/⅔ cup) sliced ginger

2 teaspoons dried yuzu pieces, or lemon zest

800 g (1 lb 12 oz) kipfler (fingerling) potatoes, sliced in half lengthways

2 bay leaves

3 peaches

2 tablespoons sugar

60 ml (2 fl oz/¼ cup) Japanese rice vinegar

serves 4

Preheat the oven to 120°C (230°F/Gas ½). To prepare the duck, discard the parson's nose and a small amount of the surrounding area to remove the oil glands. Discard the neck and giblets, if intact. Rinse the duck well, then thoroughly pat dry with paper towels. Carefully prick the skin all over by inserting a thin skewer in and under the skin at an angle almost parallel to the duck—this will prevent you from piercing the flesh.

Rub the duck all over, inside and out, with sea salt flakes and the sesame oil. Separate the garlic cloves from the head and place the unpeeled cloves inside the duck cavity, along with the ginger

slices and 1½ teaspoons of the yuzu. Place the duck, breast-side up, on a 'V' rack in a roasting tin, tucking the wings under, and roast on the middle shelf of the oven for 2½ hours. There is no need to baste during the cooking time.

Remove the duck from the oven. Increase the oven temperature to 200°C (400°F/Gas 6). Spoon the fat from the duck's roasting tin into a second roasting tin. Add the potatoes and bay leaves, toss to coat in the fat, then sprinkle with sea salt.

Pour 500 ml (17 fl oz/2 cups) water into the base of the duck's roasting tin and return to the top shelf of the oven, only when the oven has reached 200°C (400°F/Gas 6). At the same time, put the potatoes on the shelf below. Cook for 1¼ hours.

Meanwhile, cut the peaches into quarters, discarding the stone. Put the sugar, vinegar, 2 tablespoons water and the remaining yuzu pieces in a frying pan over high heat and stir until the sugar has dissolved. Bring to the boil and cook for 1 minute, or until pale gold in colour, then add the peach pieces and cook for 5 minutes, occasionally stirring carefully, until the peaches are soft but not mushy.

When the duck is crisp and golden all over, remove from the oven, cover lightly with foil and leave to rest for 10–15 minutes. Move the potatoes up to the top shelf and continue to cook for 15 minutes while you rest and carve the duck. Serve the duck with the potatoes and peaches.

This is a modern twist on an old classic. I love Béarnaise any way it is served, but this one is lighter and sweeter in flavour than the traditional version due to the addition of rice vinegar and mirin.

sansho beef with rice vinegar béarnaise

1.8 kg (4 lb) whole fillet of beef

2 teaspoons sansho pepper

½ teaspoon ground black pepper

½ teaspoon ground white pepper

2 teaspoons salt

2 tablespoons vegetable oil

350 g (12 oz/2 bunches) spring onions (scallions), cleaned and trimmed to a uniform length

béarnaise

60 ml (2 fl oz/¼ cup) Japanese rice vinegar

60 ml (2 fl oz/¼ cup) sake

60 ml (2 fl oz/¼ cup) mirin

2 spring onions (scallions), finely chopped

3 stems (not leaves) from mitsuba or flat-leaf (Italian) parsley, chopped

¼ teaspoon whole black peppercorns

4 large egg yolks

200 g (7 oz) chilled butter, cut into small dice

1 tablespoon finely chopped mitsuba or flat-leaf (Italian) parsley

serves 8–10

Tuck under the small end of the beef fillet so the end is about as thick as the large end, then tie up with kitchen string. This will promote more even cooking. Combine the sansho pepper and black and white peppers with the salt, then rub the mixture all over the beef.

Preheat the oven to 190°C (375°F/Gas 5). Heat the oil in a large frying pan over high heat and brown the beef well on all sides—cook each side for about 2 minutes, then turn. Arrange the spring onions over the base of a roasting tin and sit the beef on top of them. Cook in the preheated oven for 35–40 minutes for medium–rare, or until cooked to your liking. Rest for 10–15 minutes before slicing.

While the beef is cooking, make the Béarnaise. Combine the rice vinegar, sake, mirin, chopped spring onions, mitsuba stems and peppercorns in a small saucepan and bring to the boil over high heat. Cook for 6–7 minutes, or until reduced to about 1½ tablespoons.

Remove from the heat and strain into a heatproof bowl, then whisk in the egg yolks until smooth. Place over a small saucepan of simmering water, ensuring the water is not touching the bowl, and whisk until thick and frothy—about 2–3 minutes. Gradually whisk in the butter, piece by piece, until you have a thick, creamy sauce. Don't rush this process—it should take 8–10 minutes.

Remove from the heat, season to taste with a little salt and add a dash more vinegar if you like. Stir through the mitsuba and serve with the sliced beef and spring onions. Serve this dish with boiled baby potatoes and steamed Asian greens, green beans or asparagus.

hint: You can make the Béarnaise ahead of time and refrigerate it. Just make sure you reheat it very gently, whisking as you do so, until it is just heated, otherwise it will separate and become oily.

chicken pot pies

pastry

325 g (11½ oz/2½ cups) plain (all-purpose) flour

½ teaspoon sugar

90 g (3¼ oz) chilled butter, cut into small dice

2 tablespoons nori flakes

filling

1 teaspoon dashi granules

60 ml (2 fl oz/¼ cup) mirin

1 bay leaf

750 g (1 lb 10 oz) chicken thigh fillets, cut into
bite-sized pieces

1 streaky bacon rasher, finely chopped

50 g (1¾ oz) butter

1 leek, thinly sliced

60 g (2¼ oz/½ cup) plain (all-purpose) flour

375 ml (13 fl oz/1½ cups) cream

½ teaspoon Japanese mustard

1 tablespoon white miso

1 garlic clove, crushed

1 teaspoon sesame oil

200 g (7 oz) daikon, cut into 1 cm (½ in) dice

1 carrot, cut into 1 cm (½ in) dice

1 celery stalk, cut into 1 cm (½ in) dice

100 g (3½ oz/2 cups) shiitake mushrooms, stems
discarded, caps chopped

50 g (1¾ oz/⅓ cup) frozen peas, thawed

1 egg, beaten

makes 6

To make the pastry, sift the flour, sugar and a large pinch of salt into a bowl. Rub the butter in with your fingertips until the mixture resembles breadcrumbs. Using a flat-bladed knife, mix in the nori flakes, then gradually mix in 5–7 tablespoons iced water, using a cutting action, until the mixture forms small clumps. Gather into a ball and flatten into a disc. Cover with plastic wrap and refrigerate for about 30 minutes.

To make the filling, put the dashi granules, mirin, bay leaf and 375 ml (13 fl oz/1½ cups) water in a saucepan and bring to the boil. Add the chicken and allow to just come to the boil again. Cook for 2 minutes, or until almost cooked through, then remove with a slotted spoon, cool slightly, cover and refrigerate. Strain and reserve the cooking liquid and the bay leaf.

Sauté the bacon in a saucepan over medium heat for 1 minute, or until starting to brown. Set aside. Add half the butter and the leek and cook for 8 minutes, or until golden. Add the flour and cook for 1 minute. Gradually stir the reserved cooking liquid into the flour to form a smooth sauce. Add the cream and bay leaf and bring to the boil. Reduce to a simmer and cook for 30 minutes, stirring occasionally, until it becomes a thick white sauce. Stir in the mustard, miso and garlic. Discard the bay leaf.

Put the remaining butter and the sesame oil in a frying pan over medium–high heat, add the daikon, carrot, celery and shiitake and cook, stirring regularly, for 10–12 minutes until golden. Add the vegetables to the white sauce, along with the peas, chicken and bacon. Divide the mixture between six 375 ml (13 fl oz/1½ cup) ramekins or small ovenproof ceramic dishes and refrigerate until chilled.

Preheat the oven to 180°C (350°F/Gas 4). Divide the pastry into six equal portions, then roll out each separately between two pieces of baking paper so that they are larger in diameter than the tops of the ramekins. Remove one piece of baking paper and invert the pastry onto the top of the ramekins. Peel off the top layer and gently press the overhanging edges around the side of each dish to help adhere. Trim to neaten. Pierce the lid to form an air vent. Refrigerate for at least 20 minutes.

Brush the tops of the pies with beaten egg, avoiding the air vent, then bake for 35–40 minutes, or until the pastry is golden and the filling is heated through.

I have enjoyed many versions of this dish during my travels throughout Japan. It is basically an Italian recipe that is quite similar to lasagne, but made with rice instead of pasta. It's no wonder then that a rice-loving country like Japan would embrace it with such enthusiasm.

seafood doria

béchamel sauce
50 g (1¾ oz) butter

60 g (2¼ oz/½ cup) plain (all-purpose) flour

large pinch of freshly grated nutmeg

600 ml (21 fl oz) milk

1 bay leaf

125 ml (4 fl oz/½ cup) cream

1 tablespoon olive oil

20 g (¾ oz) butter

1 onion, finely chopped

2 streaky bacon rashers, chopped

1 garlic clove, crushed

1 small red capsicum (pepper), cut into small dice

150 g (5½ oz/1⅔ cups) shimeji mushrooms, pulled apart

16 raw medium prawns (shrimp), peeled and deveined

16 large white scallops without roe, muscle removed

2 tablespoons mirin

¼ teaspoon dashi granules

60 g (2¼ oz/¼ cup) tomato paste (purée)

1 kg (2 lb 4 oz/6 cups) cooked Japanese short-grain rice, cooled to room temperature—you will need 550 g (1 lb 4 oz/2½ cups) raw rice

3 teaspoons nori flakes

225 g (8 oz/1½ cups) grated mozzarella cheese

100 g (3½ oz/1 cup) grated Parmesan cheese

serves 6–8

To make the béchamel sauce, heat the butter in a saucepan over medium heat, add the flour and nutmeg and cook, stirring, for 1 minute. Remove from the heat and slowly whisk in the milk until smooth. Add the bay leaf and return to the heat, then stir for 10 minutes, or until the sauce thickens and coats the back of a spoon. Remove from the heat, stir in the cream and cool to room temperature. Discard the bay leaf. Season to taste.

Preheat the oven to 180°C (350°F/Gas 4). Heat half the olive oil and half the butter in a deep-sided frying pan over medium heat, add the onion and cook for 5 minutes, or until soft and lightly golden. Add the bacon, garlic, capsicum and shimeji and cook for 6–7 minutes, or until softened. Remove from the pan and set aside.

Add the remaining oil and butter to the pan and increase the heat to high. Add the prawns and sauté for 30–40 seconds, or until the prawns just turn pink. Remove and set aside with the vegetables. Allow the pan to heat up again and add a little more oil, if needed. Add the scallops and sear on each side for 30 seconds, then set aside. Add the mirin, dashi granules, tomato paste and 250 ml (9 fl oz/ 1 cup) water to the pan, stirring to scrape up any cooked sediment on the base of the pan, then bring to the boil. Remove from the heat and add the rice, seafood, vegetables and nori flakes and stir to combine well. Season.

Spoon the rice mixture into a greased 3 litre (105 fl oz/12 cup) gratin or ceramic baking dish and smooth over with the back of a spoon. Spoon the béchamel over the top. Sprinkle with the combined mozzarella and Parmesan cheeses and bake in the preheated oven for about 50 minutes, or until the rice is heated through and the top is golden and bubbling. Serve with Green salad with Japanese dressing (page 142).

side plates

Western-style green side salads are very popular in Japan today and they are almost always served with this addictive vinaigrette.

green salad with japanese dressing

100 g (3½ oz/3 cups) mixed salad leaves

175 g (6 oz/1 bunch) asparagus, lightly blanched and refreshed

8 snow peas (mangetout), lightly blanched and refreshed

1 small Lebanese (short) cucumber

1 small ripe avocado

dressing

1½ tablespoons Japanese rice vinegar

2 tablespoons Japanese soy sauce

1 tablespoon mirin

¼ teaspoon finely grated ginger

1 garlic clove, bruised

1 teaspoon caster (superfine) sugar

1½ tablespoons vegetable oil

½ teaspoon sesame oil

serves 4–6

Rinse and drain the salad leaves well, and cut large or long leaves into small bite-sized pieces. Cut the asparagus and snow peas into 3 cm (1¼ in) lengths. Cut the cucumber in half lengthways, scoop out the seeds with a teaspoon, then slice the flesh into half moons. Put in the refrigerator to chill.

Meanwhile, put all the dressing ingredients in a jar and shake well. Leave for 15 minutes to allow the flavours to develop.

When ready to serve, cut the avocado into 2 cm (¾ in) dice, then gently toss together with the salad leaves, asparagus, snow peas and cucumber. Pour over the dressing and serve immediately.

hint: Add some halved cherry tomatoes for colour or add some extra crunch by garnishing with small Japanese rice crackers or crispy wasabi peas (you can find these in your local Asian food store). To make the salad a meal, add some sliced poached or barbecued chicken.

Refreshing and tart with crisp apple and a light soy and ginger dressing, this coleslaw is a welcome change from the usual heavily mayonnaise-laden versions.

japanese coleslaw

200 g (7 oz) Chinese cabbage
1 carrot, peeled
150 g (5½ oz) daikon, peeled
2 spring onions (scallions), thinly sliced
2½ teaspoons toasted black sesame seeds
1 large Fuji apple

dressing
2 tablespoons Japanese rice vinegar
1½ tablespoons sake
¼ teaspoon Japanese mustard
½ teaspoon sesame oil
1 tablespoon Japanese soy sauce
1½ teaspoons caster (superfine) sugar
½ teaspoon finely grated ginger and its juice

serves 4–6

Finely shred the cabbage and place in a large bowl. Cut the carrot and daikon into 5 cm (2 in) lengths, then either julienne using a Japanese mandolin with the coarse-toothed comb, or coarsely grate. Put the daikon in a colander, sprinkle with salt and rest for 15 minutes. Use your hands to squeeze out any excess moisture from the daikon.

Add the daikon and carrot to the cabbage, along with the spring onions and sesame seeds. Core the apple (if preferred, you can leave the skin on for colour and extra nutrients) and julienne with the Japanese mandolin or coarsely grate. Add to the other vegetables.

Combine all the dressing ingredients and whisk until smooth. Pour over the coleslaw, season to taste and toss well to combine. Chill for 1 hour before serving. Great with fried foods.

hint: If you can't resist a creamy coleslaw dressing, add 90 g (3¼ oz/⅓ cup) Japanese mayonnaise to the dressing and stir until smooth.

Miso has many uses other than in soups. Here, this versatile ingredient is used in a delicious dressing for crisp green beans.

green beans with sesame miso dressing

250 g (9 oz) green beans, trimmed and cut into
   5 cm (2 in) lengths

dressing
50 g (1¾ oz/⅓ cup) sesame seeds
1 teaspoon sugar
2 tablespoons red or white miso
2 tablespoons mirin

serves 4–6

Bring a saucepan of lightly salted water to the boil, then add the beans and cook for 2 minutes, or until just tender. Drain, plunge into iced water until cool, then drain well.

To make the dressing, dry-fry the sesame seeds over medium heat, stirring regularly, for 5 minutes, or until lightly golden and aromatic. Immediately scoop into a mortar or *suribachi* (ribbed mortar), reserving 1 teaspoon of whole seeds for garnish, and grind until finely crushed. Gradually incorporate the sugar, miso and mirin to form a thickish paste.

Put the beans in a bowl, pour over the dressing and toss to combine. Serve in a bowl and sprinkle with the reserved sesame seeds.

hint: A *suribachi* is a Japanese mortar made from sturdy pottery. It has a ridged or textured interior designed for efficient grinding of ingredients such as sesame seeds.

Sweet corn, brushed with soy sauce and butter—what could be more simple? Great as a healthy, delicious snack and kids love them, so you might want to make a second batch.

corn batayaki

3 corn cobs, halved

30 g (1 oz) butter, melted

3 teaspoons Japanese soy sauce

2 teaspoons mirin

1 teaspoon caster (superfine) sugar

makes 6 pieces

Put the corn in a large saucepan and cover with water. Bring to the boil over high heat and cook for 3 minutes. Drain well, then put the cobs on a baking tray lined with aluminium foil.

Preheat the griller (broiler) to high. Combine the butter, soy sauce, mirin and sugar and brush liberally over the corn. Place under the griller and cook for 2–3 minutes, turning and basting regularly, until golden and slightly blistered. Brush any remaining butter mixture over the corn before serving. Sprinkle with salt and serve immediately.

hint: Try grilling (broiling) other vegetables this way. Make sure you partially cook them first if they are large pieces; smaller vegetables such as asparagus or mushrooms can go straight under the griller.

The Japanese have very successfully adopted and then adapted the humble potato salad. In Japan you find it served at the most unexpected times—at breakfast; or at lunch, neatly tapped from an ice cream scoop into a perfect mound to accompany a sandwich.

potato salad

500 g (1 lb 2 oz) all-purpose potatoes, such as desiree, peeled

50 g (1¾ oz) sliced ham

1 Lebanese (short) cucumber

dressing

175 g (6 oz/¾ cup) Japanese mayonnaise

½ teaspoon Japanese mustard

2 tablespoons Japanese rice vinegar

a few drops of sesame oil

2 spring onions (scallions), finely chopped

2 large handfuls mitsuba or flat-leaf (Italian) parsley, finely chopped, plus extra to garnish

ground white pepper

serves 6–8

To make the dressing, combine the mayonnaise, mustard, vinegar and sesame oil in a small bowl and mix until smooth, then stir in the spring onions and chopped mitsuba. Season with salt and ground white pepper.

Put the warm potato, ham, cucumber and dressing in a bowl and toss to combine well. Allow to sit for 15 minutes so the potato can absorb some of the dressing and the flavours can develop. Garnish with the extra mitsuba and serve.

Cut the potatoes into 2 cm (¾ in) dice. Bring a saucepan of salted water to the boil and add the potatoes. Cook for 8–10 minutes, or until tender. Drain, rinse under cold running water, then drain again. Crush the potatoes lightly with a fork but do not mash—there should still be some lumps.

Cut the ham into thin strips, about 3 cm (1¼ in) in length. Cut the cucumber in half lengthways, scoop out the seeds with a teaspoon, and slice the flesh very thinly.

Because daikon is so nutritious, it makes you feel a little less guilty about eating something fried and crispy.

daikon hash browns

600 g (1 lb 5 oz) daikon, peeled
1½ teaspoons grated ginger
1 small onion, very finely chopped
1 small handful mitsuba or flat-leaf (Italian) parsley,
   roughly chopped
1 egg, lightly beaten
ground white pepper
60 g (2¼ oz/⅓ cup) potato starch
30 g (1 oz/¼ cup) plain (all-purpose) flour
1½ teaspoons salt
vegetable oil, for shallow-frying

makes 10–12

Cut the daikon into three even pieces, then put the pieces in a saucepan and cover with water. Bring to the boil and cook for 25–30 minutes, or until just tender. Drain well and, when cool enough to handle, coarsely grate into a bowl lined with a tea towel. Gather the tea towel up to enclose the daikon and squeeze out any excess moisture.

Put the squeezed daikon into a clean bowl, then add the ginger, onion, mitsuba and egg, season with white pepper and combine. Mix in the potato starch, flour and the salt.

Pour enough vegetable oil into a deep-sided frying pan to come 5 mm (¼ in) up the side of the pan, then place over medium–high heat. When the oil is hot, add the mixture to the pan in heaped tablespoons, working in batches and flattening the mixture down with the back of the spoon. Cook for 2 minutes on each side, or until crisp and golden. Drain well on paper towels and serve hot as a side dish or as a snack.

Jap pumpkin has a naturally sweet flavour, which is enhanced by roasting. When mashed together with fresh ginger, it makes a wonderful accompaniment to rich roast meats such as lamb, pork or duck.

roast pumpkin and ginger mash

1.5 kg (3 lb 5 oz) jap (kent) pumpkin, seeded and
    cut into 4 even pieces
vegetable oil
sea salt flakes
100 g (3½ oz) butter, cut into small dice
¼ teaspoon sesame oil
2 teaspoons Japanese soy sauce
1½ teaspoons finely grated ginger and its juice
ground white pepper

serves 6

Preheat the oven to 200°C (400°F/Gas 6). Put the pumpkin, skin-side down, in a roasting tin, drizzle with vegetable oil and sprinkle with sea salt. Roast for 1 hour 20 minutes, or until very tender.

Scoop the flesh from the skin and place it in a bowl. Add the butter and sesame oil and mash until very smooth and lump-free. Stir in the soy sauce and ginger and juice and season with a little salt and white pepper, to taste. Reheat gently if necessary.

The addition of honey, soy sauce and a little butter to roast vegetables gives them a slight glaze and sweetness. Although daikon is normally simmered or served raw, it is a welcome addition to the roasted vegetables, giving the dish a real Japanese flavour, perfect for matching with other foods in this book.

honey soy roast vegetables

300 g (10½ oz) white sweet potato

300 g (10½ oz) orange sweet potato

300 g (10½ oz) all-purpose potatoes,
    such as desiree

600 g (1 lb 5 oz) daikon

450 g (1 lb) jap (kent) pumpkin

60 ml (2 fl oz/¼ cup) vegetable oil

1 teaspoon sesame oil

1 teaspoon sea salt flakes

1½ tablespoons honey

10 g (¼ oz) butter

3 teaspoons Japanese soy sauce

1 tablespoon sesame seeds

serves 6

Preheat the oven to 200°C (400°F/Gas 6). Peel all the vegetables except the pumpkin. Remove any seeds from the pumpkin. Cut the vegetables into even-sized pieces, about 4 x 4 cm (1½ x 1½ in). Put the pumpkin in a single layer in one roasting tin and put the other vegetables in a single layer in a second tin. Drizzle with the vegetable and sesame oils and sprinkle with sea salt. (It is a good idea to put the pumpkin in one tin as it may need to be removed from the oven earlier than the other vegetables.) Use your hands to mix the vegetables so they are lightly coated in the oil.

Put the vegetables in the oven and cook for 1 hour, or until golden and just cooked through, shaking the tins occasionally during cooking time. As the pumpkin may cook faster than the other vegetables, check after 35 minutes of cooking, remove it from the oven if cooked, and return to the oven for the last 5 minutes of cooking to heat through. Swap the tins halfway through to ensure even cooking.

Combine the honey, butter, soy sauce and sesame seeds in a small saucepan and heat over medium heat until the butter is melted and the honey is liquid. Combine all the vegetables, put them onto one of the roasting tins and drizzle with the honey mixture. Return to the oven for 10–15 minutes, shaking the tin occasionally, until the vegetables are slightly glazed and the sesame seeds are toasted. Serve with green beans to accompany a roast, or as part of a vegetarian buffet.

Creamy mash with a hint of garlic and mitsuba is perfect for accompanying richly flavoured stews and casseroles. Mitsuba, which translates as 'three leaves', is a type of Japanese parsley with a fresh, slightly peppery flavour.

mitsuba mash

1 kg (2 lb 4 oz) all-purpose potatoes, such as
    desiree, peeled and chopped
60 g (2¼ oz) butter
250 ml (9 fl oz/1 cup) cream
2 garlic cloves, crushed
3 handfuls mitsuba or flat-leaf (Italian) parsley,
    chopped

serves 6

Cook the potatoes in a large saucepan of salted boiling water for 12–15 minutes, or until tender, then drain well. Combine the butter, cream and garlic in a small saucepan and heat gently until the butter melts.

Mash the potatoes while you gradually pour in the cream mixture. Continue mashing until smooth. Stir in the mitsuba and season, to taste.

hint: Add chives or spring onions (scallions) for added flavour.

A perfect accompaniment to roasts and other savoury mains, this creamy gratin is a little lighter in texture than you might expect, thanks to the combination of daikon and potato.

daikon and potato gratin

800 g (1 lb 12 oz) daikon, peeled

1½ tablespoons salt

500 g (1 lb 2 oz) all-purpose potatoes, such as desiree, peeled

600 ml (21 fl oz) cream

5 x 10 cm (2 x 4 in) piece of kombu, wiped with a damp cloth, cut into strips

3 spring onions (scallions), bruised

2 bay leaves

2 garlic cloves, crushed

ground white pepper

serves 6–8

Using a Japanese mandolin or a very steady hand and a sharp knife, slice the daikon into very thin rounds. Toss with the salt and put in a colander over a bowl and allow to drain for 45 minutes. Slice the potatoes in the same manner, put them in a bowl and cover with cold water.

Meanwhile, put the cream, kombu strips, spring onions, bay leaves and garlic in a large saucepan and slowly bring to the boil. Remove the kombu and discard it. Boil for 2 minutes, then discard the spring onions and bay leaves and season well with salt and a little white pepper.

Rinse the daikon well, then drain again and squeeze out any excess moisture with your hands. Drain the potatoes well. Pat dry the daikon and potato slices with paper towels or a clean tea towel.

Preheat the oven to 180°C (350°F/Gas 4). Combine the daikon, potatoes and cream mixture in a bowl, then neatly layer the vegetable slices into a lightly buttered 2 litre (70 fl oz/8 cup) non-metallic gratin or baking dish. Pour over any remaining cream left in the bowl. Cover the dish tightly with foil and cook for 50 minutes, then remove the foil and cook for a further 20 minutes, or until the vegetables are tender and the top is bubbling and golden. Rest for 10 minutes before cutting into slices.

hint: Although you might be tempted, don't skip the salting step (this draws out excess liquid from the water-rich daikon), or you may end up with a rather watery mess. The starch in the potatoes helps to thicken any remaining liquid.

sweet plates

This glistening green jelly with lush fruit salad is great on its own but I can't resist teaming it with green tea ice cream for my own rendition of jelly and ice cream.

midori jelly with green fruit salad

green tea ice cream
250 ml (9 fl oz/1 cup) milk

625 ml (22 fl oz/2½ cups) cream

1 vanilla bean, roughly chopped

9 egg yolks

150 g (5½ oz/⅔ cup) caster (superfine) sugar

3 teaspoons Japanese green tea powder

jelly
150 g (5½ oz/⅔ cup) caster (superfine) sugar

a strip of lemon or lime zest

5 teaspoons gelatine powder

250 ml (9 fl oz/1 cup) Midori or other green,
    melon-flavoured liqueur

green fruit salad
3 kiwi fruit, peeled

¼ small ripe honeydew melon, peeled and seeds
    removed

175 g (6 oz/1 cup) green grapes, halved

serves 8

To make the green tea ice cream, pour the milk and cream into a saucepan, add the chopped vanilla bean, and bring just to the boil over medium–high heat. Remove the pan from the heat and allow the vanilla to infuse into the milk mixture for 15 minutes.

Put the egg yolks and sugar in a bowl and beat until creamy. Slowly pour in the milk mixture, whisking as you pour, until smooth. Pour into a clean saucepan and put the pan over medium heat. Stir for 10 minutes, or until the custard is just thick enough to coat the back of a spoon.

Put the green tea in a small bowl, stir in enough of the hot custard to form a paste, then add to the rest of the custard, whisking until smooth and an even green colour. Strain through a fine sieve and cool slightly. Cover and refrigerate until chilled.

Meanwhile, make the jelly. Put the sugar, zest and 625 ml (22 fl oz/2 ½ cups) water in a saucepan and stir over high heat until it boils. Reduce to a simmer and cook for 10 minutes. Turn off the heat.

Put the gelatine in a small bowl and stir in 60 ml (2 fl oz/¼ cup) of the hot liquid to form a smooth paste. Return to the pan and whisk until the gelatine has dissolved. Strain through a fine sieve and allow to cool. Stir in the Midori until well combined, then divide among eight tumblers or small glass bowls. Refrigerate for about 3 hours, or until set.

Remove the chilled ice cream mixture from the refrigerator and pour into an ice cream machine, then churn according to the manufacturer's instructions. Place in the freezer until ready to use. If making by hand, pour the mixture into a metal container and freeze until frozen around the edges but not in the centre, then whisk with electric beaters to break down any ice crystals. Return to the freezer and repeat this process at least twice more. The more times it is beaten while freezing, the finer and silkier the finished ice cream will be.

To make the fruit salad, cut the kiwi fruit and melon into 1.5 cm (⅝ in) dice. Place in a bowl, add the grapes and toss to combine. Spoon the fruit on top of the jelly and serve immediately with green tea ice cream.

Combine the sugar, lemon zest, ginger and 375 ml (13 fl oz/1½ cups) water in a saucepan. Stir over high heat until the sugar has dissolved, then bring to the boil. Reduce the heat to low and simmer for 10 minutes. Cool completely and strain.

Purée the plum flesh in a food processor, then strain through a fine sieve to extract the juice—about 250 ml (9 fl oz/1 cup). Add to the cooled syrup, along with the plum wine, then pour into a shallow 30 x 20 cm (12 x 8 in) metal container. Place in the freezer until the mixture begins to freeze around the edges—this will take 1½–2 hours. Scrape the frozen sections back into the mixture with a fork. Repeat every 30 minutes until the mixture has even-sized ice crystals. Just before serving, beat the mixture with a fork, then spoon into six glasses or small bowls. Serve with sliced fresh ripe plums, if desired.

hint: For a refreshing summer cocktail, serve the granita in tall glasses topped up with extra plum wine and soda, or serve in martini glasses topped with Champagne.

Japanese plum wine, *ume shu*, is a sweet wine that has an almondish flavour. It is made from *ume*, a fruit often called a plum, but actually a member of the apricot family. This sparkling pink granita is light and refreshing, perfect for the warmer summer months.

plum wine granita

115 g (4 oz/½ cup) caster (superfine) sugar
a few strips of lemon zest
2 cm (¾ in) piece young ginger, thinly sliced
500 g (1 lb 2 oz) ripe plums, seeded
500 ml (17 fl oz/2 cups) Japanese plum wine
sliced plums, extra to serve (optional)

serves 6

Melons in Japan are often seen with price tags equating to a few hundred dollars and, although exorbitantly priced, they are always beautifully gift boxed and perfect in every way—shape, colour, texture, flavour and aroma. The wonderful perfume of yuzu, a Japanese citrus, adds an exotic touch to the rockmelon, which, for most of us living outside of Japan, is an everyday food.

rockmelon and lychees with yuzu syrup

1 teaspoon dried yuzu pieces, or ½ teaspoon
   each lemon and lime zest
½ vanilla bean, thinly sliced
80 g (2¾ oz/⅓ cup) caster (superfine) sugar
½ small ripe rockmelon or other orange-fleshed
   melon, peeled and seeded
375 g (13 oz/2 cups) peeled and seeded fresh
   lychees (do this carefully to retain their shape)

serves 4

Put the yuzu, vanilla bean, sugar and 185 ml (6 fl oz/¾ cup) water in a small saucepan over high heat and stir until the sugar has dissolved. Bring to the boil, then reduce the heat and simmer for about 8 minutes, or until you have reached a thin syrup consistency. Remove from the heat and allow to cool completely.

Cut the rockmelon into 2.5 cm (1 in) cubes and carefully toss with the lychees, then pour the cooled syrup over the top. (There's no need to remove the vanilla bean as it softens in the syrup, and has a nice subtle flavour.) Refrigerate for 2–3 hours, or until well chilled. Gently stir every so often. Serve by itself or with Ginger ice cream (page 184).

ginger custard tart with toffeed strawberries

pastry

225 g (8 oz/1¾ cups) plain (all-purpose) flour

40 g (1½ oz/⅓ cup) icing (confectioners') sugar

125 g (4½ oz) frozen unsalted butter, grated

2 tablespoons black sesame seeds

1 egg yolk, beaten

custard

500 ml (17 fl oz/2 cups) cream

125 ml (4 fl oz/½ cup) milk

1 vanilla bean, split in half lengthways, seeds scraped

50 g (1¾ oz/⅓ cup) peeled, thinly sliced young ginger

8 egg yolks

80 g (2¾ oz/⅓ cup) caster (superfine) sugar

2 tablespoons plain (all-purpose) flour

2 tablespoons cornflour (cornstarch)

toffee

280 g (10 oz/1¼ cups) caster (superfine) sugar

750 g (1 lb 10 oz) strawberries, unhulled

serves 6–8

To make the pastry, sift the flour and icing sugar into a bowl. Rub the butter into the mixture until it resembles breadcrumbs. Combine the sesame seeds, egg yolk and 2½ tablespoons iced water and, using a flat-bladed knife, 'cut' into the flour mixture until it clumps. Add a little more iced water if needed. Gather into a ball and flatten slightly. Cover with plastic wrap and refrigerate for 1 hour.

To make the custard, put 375 ml (13 fl oz/1½ cups) of the cream, the milk, vanilla bean and seeds, and ginger into a saucepan and bring to the boil over medium heat. Set aside to infuse for 15 minutes. Combine the egg yolks, sugar, flour and cornflour in a large heatproof bowl and whisk until smooth.

Return the cream mixture to a medium heat, bring just to the boil again, then strain onto the eggs, whisking until smooth. Place the bowl over a saucepan of simmering water and stir continuously for 15 minutes, or until smooth and thick. Cool slightly, then press plastic wrap onto the surface of the custard and chill completely. Whip the remaining cream and fold it through the chilled custard. Chill until ready to serve.

Meanwhile, sprinkle the pastry with flour and roll out between two pieces of baking paper to 5 mm (¼ in) thick and 36 cm (14½ in) round. Trim the edges to neaten. Peel off the top layer of baking paper and invert the pastry over a 2.5 cm (1 in) deep, 28 cm (11 in) diameter loose-based tart tin and carefully press the pastry into the base. Patch any holes with excess pastry. Allow the pastry to come up 5 mm (¼ in) above the edge of the tin and pinch the edges to neaten. Refrigerate for 20 minutes.

Preheat the oven to 180°C (350°F/Gas 4). Prick the base of the pastry all over, line with baking paper and fill with baking beads or raw rice. Cook for 10 minutes, then remove the paper and weights and cook for 25 minutes, or until golden and dry to touch. Cool thoroughly in the tin on a wire rack. Only remove the tart shell from the tin when you are about to fill it with the custard.

To make the toffee, combine the sugar and 80 ml (2½ fl oz/⅓ cup) water in a saucepan. Stir with a metal spoon over medium heat until the sugar has dissolved, then bring to the boil and cook, without stirring, for 6 minutes, or until deep golden in colour (swirl the pan occasionally). Remove the pan from the heat and, holding each strawberry by the stem, carefully dip it into the hot toffee. Place the toffeed strawberries on a tray lined with baking paper to set. In humid weather the toffee will start to dissolve, so don't prepare them too far in advance. To serve, spoon the custard cream into the pastry shell, smooth over, and decorate with the strawberries.

The crisp cinnamon wafers in this recipe were inspired by a cookie, local to Kyoto, called *yatsuhashi*. These, combined with the flavour and texture of chestnuts and mandarins, make for an unusual but delicious dessert.

cinnamon wafers with chestnut cream

wafers

40 g (1½ oz/¼ cup) blanched almonds
90 g (3¼ oz/½ cup) brown rice flour
60 g (2¼ oz/½ cup) plain (all-purpose) flour
3 tablespoons roasted soya bean flour
2 tablespoons arrowroot
60 g (2¼ oz/½ cup) icing (confectioners') sugar
5 teaspoons ground cinnamon
100 g (3½ oz) chilled unsalted butter, chopped
1½ tablespoons black sugar syrup or molasses
½ teaspoon pure vanilla extract

chestnut cream

440 g (15½ oz) tin unsweetened chestnut purée
2½ tablespoons caster (superfine) sugar
2 teaspoons pure vanilla extract
1 tablespoon cognac or brandy
1 tablespoon black sugar syrup or molasses
300 ml (10½ fl oz) thickened cream, whipped

235 g (8½ oz/1 cup) tinned mandarin segments
extra black sugar syrup, for drizzling (optional)

serves 6

To make the wafers, finely grind the almonds in a food processor. Add the rice flour, plain flour, soya bean flour, arrowroot, icing sugar and cinnamon and process to combine. Add the butter and pulse until the mixture resembles breadcrumbs, then add the black sugar syrup and vanilla and pulse again until it comes together to form a smooth dough. Add a little water if needed, but only add 1 teaspoon at a time. Wrap in plastic wrap and refrigerate for 1 hour.

Preheat the oven to 180°C (350°F/Gas 4). Remove the pastry from the fridge 5 minutes before rolling it out. Meanwhile, line two baking trays with baking paper. On a lightly floured work surface, roll out the dough to about 3 mm (⅛ in) thick, sprinkling a little flour on top if the dough is a bit sticky. Using an 8 cm (3¼ in) round cookie cutter, cut out 12 circles from the dough.

Place on the lined trays (they don't spread much so you don't need to leave much space between them) and bake for 12–15 minutes, or until dark golden, but be careful as they can burn quickly at this point. Cool on the tray on a wire rack.

To make the chestnut cream, mash the chestnut purée with the sugar, vanilla, brandy and black sugar syrup until smooth, then fold through the cream and chill.

To serve, place a wafer on a serving plate and top with a large dollop of the chestnut cream and 2 tablespoons of the mandarin segments. Drizzle with the extra sugar syrup, if using, and top with a wafer 'lid'. Repeat with the remaining ingredients to make six stacks.

hint: The wafers are also great on their own and store well in sealed containers.

Japanese green tea powder, or *matcha*, is made by grinding a high-grade green tea to a fine powder. Its most common use is in traditional tea ceremonies but it is also used to flavour Japanese confectionery and desserts. It can be expensive but a little goes a long way.

green tea panna cotta with rhubarb

panna cotta
1½ teaspoons Japanese green tea powder

600 ml (21 fl oz) cream

175 g (6 oz/¾ cup) caster (superfine) sugar

3 teaspoons gelatine powder

125 ml (4 fl oz/½ cup) milk

½ teaspoon pure vanilla extract

6 large rhubarb stalks

80 g (2¾ oz/⅓ cup) caster (superfine) sugar

25 g (1 oz) unsalted butter

serves 6

To make the panna cotta, put the green tea powder in a saucepan with a little of the cream and mix to form a paste. Whisk in the remaining cream, ensuring there are no lumps. Add the sugar to the saucepan, stirring to dissolve the sugar, then slowly bring to the boil over medium heat. Turn off the heat.

Put the gelatine in a small bowl and whisk in 60 ml (2 fl oz/¼ cup) of the hot cream to form a smooth paste. Return the mixture to the saucepan, stirring until the gelatine has completely dissolved. Rest for 10 minutes to infuse the flavours and colour from the tea.

Strain into a large bowl with a pouring lip and then pour in the milk and vanilla and stir until combined. Pour the mixture into six 125 ml (4 fl oz/½ cup) moulds and chill for at least 3 hours, or until set.

Preheat the oven to 200°C (400°F/Gas 6). Remove any tough strings from the rhubarb, then cut into 5 cm (2 in) lengths. Arrange the rhubarb in a single layer in a baking dish, then sprinkle with the sugar and dot with the butter. Bake for 12–15 minutes, or until the rhubarb is slightly glazed and tender but not mushy. Remove from the heat and cool to room temperature.

If you would like to unmould the panna cotta, dip the bottom of the mould briefly into hot water, then invert the mould onto a serving plate. It should be quite wobbly. Serve with the rhubarb and spoon over some syrup.

This dish is not overly sweet, so you can really enjoy the nutty toasted sesame seeds and the lovely malty flavour of *kinako*, ground soya bean flour. Sesame seeds are believed to help reduce cholesterol, high blood pressure and stress—what better excuse do you need for dessert?

toasted sesame semi freddo

300 ml (10½ fl oz) cream

4 eggs, separated

40 g (1½ oz/⅓ cup) icing (confectioners') sugar

2 tablespoons honey

25 g (1 oz/¼ cup) roasted soya bean flour

80 g (2¾ oz/½ cup) toasted sesame seeds, lightly crushed

3 bananas, sliced on the diagonal

honey, to drizzle

serves 6–8

Whip the cream to firm peaks, then cover with plastic wrap and refrigerate until chilled. Combine the egg yolks, icing sugar and honey in a bowl and whisk for 3 minutes, or until pale and creamy. Stir in the soya bean flour and crushed sesame seeds. Fold in the chilled whipped cream.

Beat the egg whites to firm peaks, stir a large spoonful into the cream mixture, then gently fold in the rest of the whites until smooth and lump-free.

Line a 10 x 21 cm (4 x 8¼ in) loaf tin with plastic wrap, using enough plastic so that the wrap hangs over the long sides. Carefully pour the mixture into the tin, then fold the plastic over the top to cover. Freeze for 4 hours, or until frozen but not rock hard. If you make this ahead of time, remove it from the freezer about 10 minutes before cutting. Slice and serve with bananas and drizzle with honey.

hint: This is also great drizzled with chocolate sauce. Make your own sauce by gently heating 150 g (5½ oz) dark chocolate and 250 ml (9 fl oz/ 1 cup) cream until the chocolate just melts, then stir until smooth. Use Japanese chocolate if you can find it; otherwise use your favourite brand.

Azuki beans, or red beans, might seem like an unusual choice for dessert but they are used all over Japan in confectionery, often as a ready-made bean paste. These rolls are very rich, so one per person should be enough.

azuki bean, banana and chocolate spring rolls

6 large spring roll wrappers
150 g (5½ oz/½ cup) sweet azuki bean paste
3 small bananas, sliced
85 g (3 oz) good-quality dark chocolate, preferably
    Japanese, cut into 6 fingers
1 egg, lightly beaten
vegetable oil, for deep-frying

makes 6

Place a spring roll wrapper on your work surface, with a corner towards you. Put 1 tablespoon of bean paste in the lower third of the diamond and flatten slightly into a horizontal mound. Place a few slices of banana on top, slightly overlapping, then top with a finger of chocolate.

Starting at the end closest to you, roll the spring roll up and away from you, tucking in the ends halfway. Brush the final flap with a little of the beaten egg and seal. Refrigerate while you heat the oil.

Fill a deep-fat fryer or large saucepan one-third full with oil and heat to 180°C (350°F), or until a cube of bread dropped into the oil browns in 15 seconds. Cook the spring rolls for 3 minutes, or until golden. Drain on paper towels. Cool slightly, then serve with a scoop of ice cream, such as Green tea ice cream (page 164).

Toss the blueberries with the sake, sugar and lemon zest, then divide among six *chawan mushi* cups, Japanese teacups or small Chinese rice bowls, about 250 ml (9 fl oz/1 cup) capacity.

Lightly beat the eggs and egg yolks, then stir in the cream, sugar and vanilla, combining well—do not overbeat or you will aerate too much. Strain into a large bowl with a pouring lip, then pour into the teacups or bowls. Allow to sit for 10 minutes, then prick any air bubbles with a fine skewer.

Bring a wok or large saucepan filled with water to the boil, then reduce to a simmer. Put the cups in a large bamboo steamer. Wrap a clean tea towel around the steamer lid (this will collect the steam and stop any condensation from dripping onto the custards) and firmly place the lid on the steamer. Put the steamer on top of the wok and leave the custards to steam for 15–20 minutes, or until just set. If you can fit all the custards in the steamer at once, they will take the longer cooking time; if you have to do them in two batches, they will cook more quickly.

Remove from the heat and allow to cool slightly before serving. The custards can also be served chilled, but they will not have the silky texture that they have when warm.

hint: Meaning 'steamed teacups', *chawan mushi* is the name given not only to the recipe but also to the specially designed lidded, ceramic cup in which it is cooked. These may be difficult to find outside of Japan, but may be substituted with Japanese teacups or small Asian rice or soup bowls.

This sweet steamed custard was inspired by the Japanese savoury custard, *chawan mushi*. Steaming over simmering water gives the custard a silken texture, but if the water boils you will end up with a grainy mass, so take care. Like the sake that flavours it, this dish is great served warm or cold.

steamed vanilla custard cups

300 g (10½ oz/2 cups) blueberries

1½ tablespoons drinking sake

3 teaspoons caster (superfine) sugar

½ teaspoon finely grated lemon zest

4 eggs

4 egg yolks

500 ml (17 fl oz/2 cups) cream

80 g (2¾ oz/⅓ cup) caster (superfine) sugar, extra

1 teaspoon pure vanilla extract

serves 6

At one time in Tokyo, tiramisu was featured on the menu of almost every café, restaurant and fast-food chain. Like many other Italian dishes that have been adopted by the Japanese, it has been made their own by substituting flavours that are more familiar to them. This version is quite a leap from the original.

tokyo tiramisu

300 g (10½ oz) good-quality white chocolate, chopped
500 ml (17 fl oz/2 cups) cream
¾ teaspoon Japanese green tea powder, plus extra to serve
55 g (2 oz/¼ cup) caster (superfine) sugar
325 ml (11 fl oz) drinking sake
22 large savoiardi biscuits, cut in half lengthways
500 g (1 lb 2 oz/1½ cups) sweet azuki bean paste
extra white chocolate

serves 8–10

Combine the chocolate and cream in a saucepan and stir over low heat until almost melted. Remove from the heat and stir until completely lump-free. Add a little of the mixture to the green tea powder in a small bowl and stir to make a smooth runny paste. Pour this back into the chocolate mixture and stir until smooth and evenly coloured. Pour through a very fine sieve into a bowl, pressing down on any lumps of tea with the back of a spoon to extract the flavour and colour. The cream may still be slightly speckled, which is fine. Cover and refrigerate for 4 hours, or until completely cold.

When cold, whip the chocolate cream until just spreadable—be careful not to overbeat the mixture as it may split—then refrigerate until ready to use.

Combine the sugar with 170 ml (5½ fl oz/⅔ cup) water and stir over high heat until the sugar has dissolved. Allow to boil for 2 minutes, then remove the pan from the heat, cool completely and mix in the sake. Dip half the sponge fingers into the syrup, one at a time, and use them to line the base of a 6–7 cm (2½–2¾ in) deep, 2.5 litre (87 fl oz/10 cup) capacity serving dish.

Using half the azuki bean paste, drop spoonfuls over the sponge fingers and gently spread out with the back of a spoon, trying not to move the savoiardi. Spread half the green tea chocolate cream over this and smooth over.

Repeat the layering with the sponge, syrup, bean paste and chocolate cream and smooth the top with a palette knife so that it is as flat as possible. Finely grate the extra white chocolate over the top, ensuring the surface is evenly and completely covered. Carefully cover with plastic wrap and refrigerate overnight to allow the flavours to develop. Do not store in the refrigerator with any other strong flavours. Sprinkle with the extra green tea powder. Serve in small portions as this is a very sweet dessert.

hint: If you prefer, layer the tiramisu using fresh raspberries instead of the bean paste, which will help to cut the sweetness.

Nashi is a type of pear with a crisp flesh, similar to that of an apple. Its sweet, refreshing flavour blends beautifully with the slightly spicy ice cream.

nashi strudel with ginger ice cream

ginger ice cream
250 ml (9 fl oz/1 cup) milk
630 ml (22 fl oz) cream
1 vanilla bean, split, seeds scraped and reserved
150 g (5½ oz/1¼ cups) thinly sliced young ginger
9 egg yolks
140 g (5 oz/⅔ cup) caster (superfine) sugar

4 nashi, peeled and quartered, core removed,
    then cut into 5 mm (¼ in) thick slices
2 teaspoons lemon juice
2 teaspoons finely grated ginger
235 g (8½ oz/1 cup) caster (superfine) sugar
30 g (1 oz/½ cup) Japanese breadcrumbs
80 g (2¾ oz/½ cup) toasted sesame seeds,
    lightly ground
80 g (2¾ oz/¾ cup) walnuts, finely chopped
2 teaspoons ground cinnamon
1 teaspoon ground ginger
18 sheets filo pastry
150 g (5½ oz) unsalted butter, melted
3 tablespoons icing (confectioners') sugar
3 tablespoons roasted soya bean flour

serves 6

To make the ginger ice cream, put the milk, cream, vanilla bean and seeds and ginger in a saucepan over medium–high heat. Bring just to the boil, then remove from the heat and set aside for 20 minutes to allow the vanilla to infuse into the milk. Strain, reserving the vanilla bean.

Put the egg yolks and sugar in a bowl and beat until the eggs are light and creamy. Whisk in the cream mixture until smooth, then pour into a clean saucepan and return to a medium heat. Add the reserved vanilla bean and stir for 10 minutes, or until the mixture just coats the back of a spoon. Strain through a fine sieve and cool slightly. Cover and refrigerate until cold, then churn in an ice cream machine, according to the manufacturer's instructions. Freeze until ready to use.

If making the ice cream by hand, pour the mixture into a metal container and freeze until it is frozen around the edges but not in the centre, then whisk with electric beaters to break down any ice crystals. Return to the freezer and repeat this process at least twice more.

Preheat the oven to 180°C (350°F/Gas 4). Put the nashi in a bowl with the lemon juice, ginger, half the sugar, and the breadcrumbs and stir. Combine the sesame seeds, remaining sugar, walnuts, cinnamon and ground ginger in a small bowl.

Lay one sheet of filo on the work surface, with the short end towards you, and brush lightly with the melted butter, then butter another sheet and place it directly on top of the first. Repeat with a third sheet, brushing the top as well. Sprinkle one-sixth of the sesame mixture over the top, then, leaving a 5 cm (2 in) border on the edge of the pastry closest to you and on both sides, put one-sixth of the nashi mixture in a neat bundle. Gently roll it up, folding in the sides about halfway, brushing more butter down each folded side. Carefully transfer to a lightly greased baking tray, seam-side down, and brush all over with melted butter. Repeat with the remaining filo and filling to form six strudels. Bake for 35 minutes, or until crisp and golden. Allow to cool slightly, then slice the ends off to expose the filling. Sift over the combined icing sugar and soya bean flour and serve with the ginger ice cream, or with lightly whipped cream.

Jap pumpkin has a rich sweet flesh, so it is little wonder the Japanese have such a fondness for it in desserts. *Kabocha*, or pumpkin, is found in many sweet foods such as puddings, pies and ice creams. Here I have used it to flavour cheesecake, which is now a staple on most Japanese café and restaurant menus.

pumpkin cheesecake

500 g (1 lb 2 oz) jap (kent) pumpkin, peeled and
   roughly chopped
175 g (6 oz) hard ginger biscuits
40 g (1½ oz/¼ cup) toasted sesame seeds, crushed
50 g (1¾ oz/½ cup) walnuts, chopped
2 tablespoons caster (superfine) sugar
80 g (2¾ oz) unsalted butter, melted
1½ tablespoons gelatine powder
600 g (1 lb 5 oz) cream cheese, softened
300 g (10½ oz) sour cream
175 g (6 oz/1 cup) loosely packed soft brown sugar
2 teaspoons pure vanilla extract
1½ teaspoons ground cinnamon
1½ teaspoons finely grated orange zest
lightly whipped cream, to serve

pumpkin and sesame seed toffee (optional)
30 g (1 oz/¼ cup) toasted unsalted pepitas
   (pumpkin seeds)
2 tablespoons toasted sesame seeds
350 g (12 oz/1½ cups) caster (superfine) sugar

serves 10–12

Cook the pumpkin in a saucepan of boiling water for 20 minutes, or until very tender. Drain well, mash and cool completely.

Break the biscuits into small pieces, then pulse with the sesame seeds, walnuts and sugar in a food processor until even crumbs are formed. Add the melted butter and mix until combined. Press into the greased and lined base of a 23 cm (9 in) springform tin and smooth over with the back of a spoon. Refrigerate until needed.

Sprinkle the gelatine over 60 ml (2 fl oz/¼ cup) warm water in a small bowl. Leave until spongy—do not stir. Bring a small saucepan of water to the boil, remove from the heat and put the bowl in the pan. The water in the pan should come only halfway up the side of the bowl—tip out a little water if necessary. Stir the gelatine until clear and dissolved.

Put the cream cheese, sour cream, brown sugar, vanilla, cinnamon and orange zest in a food processor and mix until smooth and lump-free, then add the pumpkin and gelatine and process again until smooth. Pour the mixture into the prepared tin and smooth the top. Refrigerate for 6 hours, or overnight, until set.

To make the pumpkin and sesame seed toffee, if using, line a baking tray with baking paper and sprinkle over the toasted seeds. Put the sugar and 60 ml (2 fl oz/¼ cup) water in a small saucepan, place over high heat, stir until the sugar dissolves, then bring to the boil. Cook for 8 minutes, or until deeply golden, swirling occasionally to help distribute the colour, then immediately and carefully pour over the seeds on the tray. Using protection from the heat for your hands, gently tilt and swirl the tray so that the toffee covers the seeds. Allow to cool completely before breaking into small shards. To serve, top the cheesecake with whipped cream and the toffee.

glossary

azuki bean A small red bean often used to make *an*, a sweet bean paste made by slowly cooking azuki beans in a sugar syrup.

bamboo shoots *(takenoko)* The young, pale shoots of certain bamboo, which have a mellow flavour. Sometimes available fresh, but require preparation. The precooked, tinned ones only need to be drained and rinsed before use.

black sugar *(kurozato)* A dark brown sugar with a rich molasses flavour, sold in small lumps or crushed. Used mainly in confectionery, particularly for making a sweet black sugar syrup called *kuromitsu*.

bonito flakes *(katsuobushi)* Shavings of dried, smoked and cured bonito, a type of tuna. The large flakes are used for making stock (dashi); smaller flakes are used as a garnish. It has a strong aroma but a smoky, mellow flavour.

burdock root *(gobo)* A long, brown-skinned root with a creamy coloured flesh. Available fresh when in season. To prepare, scrape off the skin, then rinse. Slice and soak in acidulated water to remove any bitterness. Some recipes ask for the root to be shaved. To do this, start at the thin end of the root and, using a sharp knife, shave off pieces as if sharpening a pencil. Frozen lengths are sold in Asian food stores. These are scraped and ready to cook.

daikon A giant radish resembling a very large white carrot. Its flavour when raw is fresh and mild, and it is used in salads or grated into dipping sauces. When cooked, it becomes a little sweet and is great in stews and stir-fries, or roasted. Daikon have a high water content and become soft and bitter with age. As they are very porous, wrap in plastic wrap and refrigerate to store.

dashi granules Dehydrated granules of the essential Japanese base stock, dashi. Also available in powdered form. Made from kombu (kelp) and dried, smoked bonito tuna, dashi forms the base for many dishes, most famously miso soup but also stews, hotpots, noodle soups and salad dressings.

enoki These mushrooms have long, thin, creamy white stems and tiny caps. They grow in clumps, attached by a spongy root that needs to be cut off before use, and can be pulled apart. They require very little cooking, if any.

ginkgo nuts *(ginnan)* Native to China, this pale yellow fruit from the *Ginkgo biloba* tree has a crisp shell when fresh, which must be removed before cooking. Commonly found ready-prepared in tins, vacuum-packed or frozen. When cooked, they develop a creamy, nutty flavour and slightly chewy texture.

harusame noodles Meaning 'spring rain', these thin, clear noodles are authentically made from bean starch, but can also be made from potato or sweet potato starch.

hijiki A porous seaweed, high in fibre and calcium. Sold dried in short lengths, which need to be reconstituted before eating.

Japanese breadcrumbs *(panko)* Crisp breadcrumbs available in fine and coarse grades. Usually larger than traditional breadcrumbs, they make a very crisp coating for deep-fried foods. The coarser grade is used for the recipes in this book.

Japanese green tea powder *(matcha)* A fine powder made by grinding high-grade green tea. It is the essential element of the Japanese tea ceremony, and is whisked with hot water before drinking. Also used to flavour desserts and some soba noodles.

Japanese mayonnaise A creamy mayonnaise with a slightly salty, sweet flavour, containing soya bean oil and rice vinegar. A popular brand is QP (for 'kewpie', the name of the doll on the label). Sold in a soft squeeze bottle for easy use.

Japanese mustard *(karashi)* A very hot and spicy yellow mustard, similar to English mustard. Use sparingly.

Japanese pickled plum *(umeboshi)* Made from *ume*, which is actually not a plum but a member of the apricot family. The fruit is pickled in salt and vinegar and coloured a deep pink-red by the red shiso leaf. Served as a tart accompaniment to rice and other foods, or desalted and used in dressings.

Japanese rice vinegar *(komesu)* Made from vinegar and a natural rice extract, this refreshing vinegar is less sharp than other types. Japanese rice vinegar has a milder, sweeter flavour than other rice vinegars, so choose a Japanese brand when cooking Japanese food.

Japanese soy sauce *(shoyu)* A high-grade soy sauce used in cooking and as a condiment. There are several good brands available and some versions are saltier or sweeter than others. The recipes in this book generally use the less sweet, lighter version, which has a more savoury flavour, but you can substitute the Japanese soy sauce of your choice.

kamaboko A small loaf of steamed fish paste made from a variety of mild-fleshed fish and tasting a little like crab sticks. It is sometimes coloured bright pink for festival foods; the regular version is a creamy white colour. Used in soups and stews.

kombu Also called konbu, this dried kelp is essential for making dashi. It can turn bitter if cooked for too long, so is often soaked overnight in the cooking liquid and then discarded. Sold in strips about 5 cm (2 in) wide from which lengths can be cut with scissors. Wipe over it with a damp cloth to remove any grit before cooking but do not rub off the white powdery substance that coats the surface.

kuzu A thickening starch added to sauces to help them glaze well, also used to set foods and to make certain noodles. Sold as a powder or as small rocks, which need to be crushed before use. Kuzu is often labelled, or substituted with, arrowroot.

lotus root *(renkon)* A rhizome rather than a root, with a crisp texture and delicate flavour. It has small holes throughout its length, which, when sliced into rounds, look like a flower. Fresh lotus root must be peeled and cooked before eating. Also available prepared and ready for cooking in tins, vacuum packs and frozen.

mirin A pale gold spirit-based rice liquid sometimes referred to as sweet rice wine. Manufactured for cooking, not drinking, and used in sauces, dressings and simmered dishes. To avoid imitations, look for bottles labelled *hon mirin*, meaning 'true mirin'.

miso A rich, earthy paste made from fermented soya beans, available in different grades, colours and strengths. Generally, the lighter the paste the sweeter and less salty the taste. Used in miso soup, but also added to other soups, marinades, dressings and simmered dishes. Two types are used in this book: white, or *shiro*, miso has a mild, sweet flavour; and red, or *aka*, miso has more earthy, salty characteristics. Often confusingly labelled, so please note that white miso is actually pale gold in colour and red miso is more a caramel brown.

mitsuba Translated as 'three leaves', this herb is a type of Japanese parsley. Similar in appearance to a cross between coriander (cilantro) and flat-leaf (Italian) parsley. If not in season, substitute flat-leaf (Italian) parsley.

mizuna A large-leafed herb with a slight peppery mustard flavour, used in salads and sometimes in simmered dishes. If not in season it can sometimes be substituted with rocket (arugula).

nashi A type of Japanese pear, more closely resembling the shape of an apple. The flesh is crisp, refreshing and sweet, and the skin is slightly rough and either pale yellow-green or brown. Browner-skinned nashi have a richer, more caramel flavour.

nori Crisp paper-like sheets of compressed seaweed, commonly used to wrap sushi, and sold in pre-cut toasted sheets for this purpose. Small strips and flakes of nori, aonori, are frequently used as a condiment or garnish.

pickled ginger (gari) Thinly sliced fresh, young ginger that turns pale pink during the pickling process. It has a sharp yet sweet and refreshing flavour, which is great as a palate cleanser for rich foods such as sashimi, which uses fatty fish, or deep-fried foods. Avoid the inferior darker pinkish-red strips that are tinted with food colouring as these have a less refined flavour.

plum wine (umeshu) A sweet liquor with a bitter almond flavour made from a type of Japanese apricot, ume.

ponzu A dressing or dipping sauce made from citrus juice, soy sauce and bonito flakes that is available commercially. To make your own, see page 16.

potato starch A starch used to thicken sauces and to coat deep-fried foods for a very crisp result.

sake An alcoholic liquid made from the fermenting of cooked, ground rice. It has a clean, dry flavour, somewhere between vodka and dry sherry. There are various grades: the more refined, clear liquid is for drinking; the less refined form, pale amber in colour, is for cooking. In this book, recipes using sake refer to cooking sake unless specified as drinking sake. Served chilled in summer and warmed in winter.

sansho pepper The ground seeds of the Japanese prickly ash. Its spicy aroma and flavour and slightly numbing quality demonstrate its close relation to Chinese Sichuan pepper. It is one of the spices that make up seven-spice mix.

soba noodles Made from buckwheat flour, these grey-brown noodles have a slightly nutty flavour and are often served chilled with a soy-based dipping sauce, or hot in broth. Available in dried form and sometimes flavoured with green tea, cha soba.

seaweed paste (nori tsukudani) A black paste made from kelp with a sweet, yet salty, mellow flavour.

seven-spice mix (shichimi togarashi) A spice mix containing seven flavours. It always includes togarashi, a hot red Japanese chilli. The remaining ingredients are flexible but often include mustard seeds, sesame seeds, poppy seeds, sansho pepper, shiso and nori flakes.

sesame oil Strongly flavoured oil extracted from toasted sesame seeds. A spicy version infused with chilli is popular for sprinkling over noodle soups. Use sparingly.

sesame seeds (goma) Usually white or cream, but also black. The oil-rich seeds are often toasted to enhance their flavour. To toast the seeds, put them in a small frying pan over low heat for 10 minutes, shaking the pan, or until golden and fragrant.

shiso Also known as perilla or beefsteak plant, this large-leafed, aromatic herb has slightly ragged edges and a flavour similar to basil or Thai basil, with which it can be substituted if unavailable. Usually dark green in colour, or with a purplish red hue. Used in salads, soups and as a garnish, it is also a popular tempura ingredient.

shiitake This mushroom has a unique, relatively strong flavour and is available both fresh and dried. The more pungent dried version is similar in appearance to the Chinese dried mushroom with which it may be substituted.

shimeji This mushroom grows in a cluster of long stems and has small grey-brown caps. It is often pulled apart before use. Delicately flavoured, it is eaten raw in salads, or briefly cooked in soups, stews or stir-fries.

shochu A distilled spirit with a high alcohol content, made from potato, sweet potato or various grains. Quality shochu is very smooth with a vodka-like flavour.

somen Fine, white wheat-flour noodles most commonly eaten chilled with a dipping sauce or warm in a light broth.

soya bean flour, roasted (kinako) A flour made from ground, roasted soya beans, it has a slightly sweet, nutty flavour. Commonly used when making traditional Japanese confectionery or desserts.

soya beans Available dried as small yellowish oval beans that require soaking before use, precooked in tins, or fresh or frozen in the pod (edamame). Rich in protein and used in the manufacture of tofu, miso and soy sauce.

tamari A naturally fermented, thick, dark and sweet Japanese soy sauce. True tamari is wheat-free, but there are some lesser quality brands that have misapplied the name, so check labels carefully if this is an important consideration.

taro A starchy tuber with a creamy, slightly nutty flavour when cooked. It must be cooked before eating.

tofu Also known as bean curd, this creamy flavoured, high-protein food is made by setting the 'milk' that results when soya beans and water are ground together. Available in a variety of textures: silken, a very soft, fragile tofu used in dressings or desserts; silken firm is slightly more set and added to light soups or salads; cotton (firm) tofu is a dense, textured tofu that holds together well for stir-fries and stews.

udon Thick, white, wheat-flour noodles available in various widths, fresh and dried. Usually served in soups, hotpots or stir-fries.

wakame A curly-leafed seaweed, usually dehydrated and broken into very small pieces. It swells considerably and quickly when added to water and has a soft texture, which can become slimy if left to soak for too long. Use in soups and salads.

wasabi Wasabi paste is a hot, pungent mixture made from the knobbly green root of the Japanese wasabi plant. It is also available in powdered form to be mixed to a paste when needed. Also available fresh when in season. The root can be finely grated and has better flavour and less heat than the paste. Use sparingly as a condiment for sushi and sashimi, and in dipping sauces for noodles.

yakisoba Chinese-style yellow egg noodles that are partially cooked and ready for use in the stir-fried noodle dish of the same name. You can substitute with thin hokkien (egg) noodles.

yuzu An aromatic Japanese citrus fruit. It is the rind, either fresh or dried, which is used more frequently than other parts of the fruit. Yuzu is used in soups and simmered dishes for added flavour and aroma. The juice is added to dipping sauces or dressings.

index